The Pooh Perplex

Frederick C. Crews

The Pooh Perplex

A Student Casebook

*In Which It is Discovered that the
True Meaning of the Pooh Stories
is Not as Simple as is Usually Believed,
But for Proper Elucidation Requires the
Combined Efforts of Several Academicians
of Varying Critical Persuasions*

ROBIN CLARK

Published by Robin Clark Limited 1979
A member of the Namara Group
27/29 Goodge Street, London W1P 1FD

Reprinted 1982 and 1984

First published in Great Britain
by Arthur Barker Ltd 1964

Printed in Great Britain by Nene Litho
and bound by Woolnough Bookbinding,
both of Wellingborough, Northants

ISBN 0 86072 026 8

Contents

Preface

Winnie-the-Pooh is, as practically everyone knows, one of the greatest books ever written, but it is also one of the most controversial. Nobody can quite agree as to what it really means! This is why it will be an ideal book around which to organize all your work in Freshman English this semester. Like other casebooks, such as those on Harper's Ferry, Edith Wharton, and the personality adjustment difficulties of Poe and Ezra Pound, this one is frankly designed to keep you in confusion. Try as you may, you will find it impossible to decide which of the critics represented has "the word" about *Pooh*, and thus, as you read one critic after another and write many papers comparing their various approaches, you will find that the course has come to an end before you scarcely realize it is under way. By that time, though, you will be a good bit wiser than you are now. No longer will you be inclined to "believe everything you read," as the saying goes. Quite the contrary! When your instructor has finished showing you how each of these essays contradicts the others, you will be likely to say, with jesting Pilate, "What is truth?" The answer is not easy to seek out, but with the question always in mind you will find much intellectual excitement in your four-year period as an undergraduate; and if at the end of that time you have not accepted some halfway answer or given up the quest, you can pass on to graduate school, becoming more and more broad-minded as time goes by.

Of course, you should not undertake this semester's work in an altogether somber spirit of "agonizing reappraisal." This book has been designed around the idea that a Freshman English course can be good fun for all the students. Your instructor will let you know which essays are the "real howlers," and you can "have a ball" discovering the misconceptions and fallacies in them. Also, please do not approach the Questions and Study Projects in a hang-dog, negativistic spirit. When you find a topic that fascinates you, why not get the whole gang together in your dorm for a bull session, and "kick the ball around" for a while? You will find it possible to "get a bang" out of developing your communications skills.

FREDERICK C. CREWS

University of California
Berkeley, California

The Pooh Perplex

HARVEY C. WINDOW

was a graduate student at the University of Pennsylvania when he wrote "Paradoxical Persona." Its publication earned him an instructorship at Indiana, where he teaches Freshman English and Second Half of the Eighteenth Century. Mr. Window would seem to be one of the truly promising younger critics. His recent casebook, What Happened at Bethlehem, *has been adopted and endorsed by a variety of institutions, from Citrus Junior College to Manayunk Teachers'.*

Paradoxical Persona:
The Hierarchy of Heroism in
Winnie-the-Pooh

HARVEY C. WINDOW

N O ONE in these days, I feel sure, will care to complain that there is a lack of critical attention to *Winnie-the-Pooh*. It is true that the book is of such quality that no amount of criticism could exhaust it, and equally true that our ideal in English studies is to amass as much commentary as possible upon the literary work, so as to let the world know how deeply we respect it. Still, A. A. Milne is well ahead of the other great children's writers in the acclaim he has received. The present proliferation, not only of *Pooh* coloring books, *Pooh* dolls, *Pooh* tablemats, *Pooh* murals, and translations into many languages ancient and modern, but also of sound critical studies, ensures the book's status as a permanent classic. Among the criticism one must stand in particular admiration of the pioneering works by Ogle, Smythe,

Bunker, and Wart.[1] No subsequent treatment of *Pooh*, including the present one, can afford to pass by the profound discoveries of these scholars.

It is, then, with a sense of my own temerity—if not, indeed, of outright rashness—that I must assert that Ogle, Smythe, Bunker, and Wart have completely missed the point of *Pooh*. Valuable as their studies have been in establishing certain connections and parallels that other scholars might not have thought were worth pursuing, I cannot honestly say that we have learned anything significant from them. Neither Ogle, nor Smythe, nor Bunker, nor Wart asked himself the absolutely basic questions about *Winnie-the-Pooh*, and thus each of them necessarily failed to grasp the key to the book's entire meaning. I find myself in the embarrassing position of being the only possessor of this key, and I am writing this essay only to alter such an unbalanced situation as quickly as possible.

Let us say at the outset that, if all great literature is more complex than the naïve reader can suspect, it is equally true that this complexity, once discovered, can be rendered in simple terms. Caroline Spurgeon's reduction of Shakespeare's imagery to certain recurrent patterns is a case in point; one could only have hoped that such an important matter could have been revealed to us with more taste, wit, intelligence, and style. (I myself had already noticed most of the patterns before reading Spurgeon, by the way.) Again, Professor Lovejoy's

1 See Bertrand Ogle, "Poohsticks as Play Therapy," *Health*, V (April, 1940); P. P. Smythe, "Piglet's Day as Roo: The 'Circe' Episode in *Winnie-the-Pooh*," *Modern Fiction Studies*, Special *Pooh* Number, VIII (January, 1956); Hans Bunker, "*Winnie-der-Pooh* als kindische Erzählung," *JEGP*, XX (December, 1958); and Harry Wart, "*Winnie-the-Pooh* as Myth, Symbol, Ritual, and Archetype," *Mandala*, I (April, 1961).

demonstration of the importance of the Great Chain of Being in Renaissance literature, while somewhat over-stated and self-evident, did have the virtue of reducing complexities to simplicities. The consequences have been, on the whole, not unfruitful, though there may be room for differences of opinion on this point. The reader, then, will not suspect the present essay of super-ficiality simply because it offers an almost formulaically simple clue to *Pooh*.

What is the purpose, the inner necessity, of *Winnie-the-Pooh*? Is it merely to recount little episodes that will engage the attention of small children? Obviously not, for the stories *as stories* are, as Smythe justly pointed out before his own article deteriorated into misleading com-parisons between Milne and Joyce, notably lacking in elements of the violent, the fabulous, the quickly thrilling. A *précis* of any chapter might cause us to wonder whether the book has any appeal whatsoever: a toy bear and a toy pig follow their own tracks around a tree until they are told by a small boy that this is pointless, and all retire for lunch. It is clear, I think, that *Pooh* must address us on an essentially subliminal level—that it must achieve its effects through sly manipulations and secret implications, not through what it directly narrates. That Bunker and the others did not perceive this is, I must say, a fact that might almost lead us to question their professional com-petence, were we not so grateful for their pioneering work.

The fatal mistake that has been made by every previous Poohologist is the confusion of Milne the writer with Milne the narrator, and of Christopher Robin the listener with Christopher Robin the character. These are not two personages but four, and no elementary understanding of

Pooh is possible without this realization. We must designate, then, the Milne *within* the story as "the Milnean voice," and we must call the Christopher Robin who listens "the Christophoric ear." With these distinctions in mind, *Pooh* begins to make perfect sense for the first time. The real A. A. Milne is writing a book in which he, translated into the Milnean voice, is to narrate stories for the edification and amusement of his son, or rather of his son-in-the-role-of-listener, the Christophoric ear. These stories will have to do with various characters, among whom will be "Christopher Robin"—not Milne's actual son, nor yet the Christophoric ear, but a character whose features and actions are determined by what Milne wants the Milnean voice to decide will be best for the Christophoric ear to emulate. Or, to be even more precise, this character, Christopher Robin, will be treated partly in a manner meant to edify the Christophoric ear, and partly in a manner demanded by that ear in order to flatter its own egoistic conception of itself. This simple notion, like Einstein's $e = mc^2$ (though perhaps less important, of course), contains the fundamental law governing *Pooh*'s fictional universe.

The heart of the matter is revealed in the opening chapter, "We Are Introduced"—the "We," I take it, referring to four personages, the Milnean voice, the Christophoric ear, Christopher Robin, and Pooh.

"What about a story?" said Christopher Robin [the Christophoric ear is speaking].

"*What* about a story?" I [the Milnean voice] said.

"Could you very sweetly tell Winnie-the-Pooh one?"

"I suppose I [see above] could," I said. "What sort of stories does he like?"

"About himself. Because he's *that* sort of Bear."

Now, "*that* sort of Bear" is of course a bear who wants to be flattered, and it is plain that the Christophoric ear is using Pooh to make its own devious request that it (the ear's projection, "Christopher Robin") be made the center of attention. The Milnean voice, however, in its didactic-paternal role, is unprepared *simply* to feed the self-love of the Christophoric ear; it (the voice) must also see that it (the ear) is properly edified in a moral sense. The stories, therefore, will express a vector of the two forces, *pleasing* and *teaching* the Christophoric ear. At the same time, I should add, A. A. Milne himself, the real author, is employing a device parallel to that of the Christophoric ear. He conceals his own desire to publish a book by making himself appear simply as the reluctantly obliging father (the Milnean voice) who must humor his son with stories, and whose stories, indeed, lie open to the direction of that son, nay, of that son's teddy bear. False modesty and literary ingenuity have rarely found so happy a union as this.

The reader will now, I trust, be rather less disposed than formerly to accept Bunker's unwary description of *Pooh* as a "*ganz einfaches Beispiel der Kinderliteratur*"; nor will he imagine, with Ogle, that the essence of the book lies in the "interpenetrating relationships of co-operation and competition" among the characters. One may hope that the hour for such critical somnolence has now passed. I shall say nothing of Wart's theory that Pooh is an Orphic deity with seasonal-sacrificial-re-demptive crop-growing characteristics—a clever idea, but one that is given a disproportionate weight in Wart's sense of the total meaning of the book. One must handle all preconceived patterns of meaning very gently to do justice to a work as subtle, as darkly double, as *Pooh*.

Armed with our interpretive key—the knowledge that all the "harmless," "happy-go-lucky" stories in the book are really dictated by compromises between the edificatory wishes of the Milnean voice and the self-indulging wishes of the Christophoric ear—we can easily discover the second, concomitant principle that knits the episodes together. This is the principle of the Hierarchy of Heroism, a chain of authority not unlike Lovejoy's Chain of Being, only more strictly operative, more functional, and more real. A. A. Milne, like Lovejoy's God, rules the Hierarchy; he has absolute control over what will happen in *Pooh*. A certain amount of power, however, is delegated to the Milnean voice, which in turn grants considerable privilege to the Christophoric ear. No one of these figures can accomplish anything without the consent of the next superior in the chain. The chain continues downward to Christopher Robin (the character) and thence to Pooh, Christopher's favorite animal. Piglet, as Pooh's best friend, comes next; weak and timid though he is, he automatically merits a place of honor by virtue of Pooh's handing-on of the Milnean *mana* to him. It is this *mana*, more than any personal virtue or effort, that accounts for his high degree of success in the adventures and enterprises he shares with Pooh. Other characters, such as Owl and Rabbit, try vainly to dominate the action, but are foredoomed to failure by their low rating. At the bottom of the order of main characters is Eeyore, the archetypal outsider; and below Eeyore extends a vast string of virtually vegetal nonentities, concluding with Rabbit's least imposing friends-and-relations, Small and Alexander Beetle.

Now, this Hierarchy, like everything else in *Pooh*, reflects a marriage of interests between the Milnean voice and the Christophoric ear. The animals near the top are alleged to be the Christophoric ear's favorites, and so they are; but the Milnean voice gives them traits of humility, spontaneity, enthusiasm, and obedience which it (the voice) hopes that it (the ear) will cultivate in its own life. Thus, when Pooh turns out to be more successful in one episode than Rabbit is, the Milnean voice is saying in effect, "Look, Christophoric ear: the meek shall inherit the earth"; while the Christophoric ear, for its part, is content to see Christopher Robin enter the episode at the end to set all wrongs right again. A little didacticism, a little egoism: that is the rationale of *Winnie-the-Pooh*'s plot.

As for illustrating these principles, we have an *embarras de richesses*, for literally everything in the book depends on them. We may, however, choose one especially complex scene in which, because of Christopher Robin's participation in the main action, the Hierarchy of Heroism is on view in its completest form. This is the so-called Expotition to the North Pole—archly dismissed by Bunker as a picaresque expression of the "*Wanderlust der Kindheit*." Future Poohians, when they have pondered the full intricacy of this scene, may well blush for Bunker's naïveté and learn from his example that a work of literature must be approached with one's critical armor riveted firmly on.

The sentence introducing the Expotition chapter is full of portentous meaning: "One fine day Pooh had stumped up to the top of the Forest to see if his friend Christopher Robin was interested in Bears at all." It takes no child psychologist to see that Pooh feels neglected and is asking himself whether his priority in Christopher Robin's Hierarchy has slipped. This, Milne implicitly informs us,

is to be a tale which will really have to do not with finding or not finding a piece of wood, but with a more or
less savage emotional free-for-all over Hierarchical rank.
Shepard's drawing of Pooh ostensibly "helping" Christopher Robin with his boot is emblematic of the chapter's

theme: Pooh and Christopher are sitting back to back,
pressing against each other with all their might. This impression is heightened by the equivocal sarcasm with
which Rabbit, the power-seeker, greets Pooh's organiza-
tional instructions, and by the pell-mell confusion of all
the animals gathered together; it is evident that no one
intends to take a servile role in the Expotition. Yet the
Expotition is to be nothing other than a symbolic ordering
of the Hierarchy; it is, in Christopher Robin's definition,
"a long line of everybody." Precisely because this ordering starts from chaos, we can take the net outcome of
this chapter as Milne's accurate word on the real constitution of the Hierarchy.

We must, however, draw an essential distinction, missed
by all previous critics, between a superficial and temporary order and the intrinsic, permanent one. Literalistic
readers, if they had perceived the Hierarchy of Heroism
at all, would doubtless have been misled by such cunning
sentences as the following: "First came Christopher
Robin and Rabbit, then Piglet and Pooh; then Kanga,

with Roo in her pocket, and Owl; then Eeyore; and, at the end, in a long line, all Rabbit's friends-and-rela-tions." The true order is of course distorted here by Rabbit's ambition and Pooh's modesty—traits that will receive their merited rewards only in the *dénouement* of the plot. How the literalists could have failed to see this is quite beyond me. A few moments later, in the "hush-ing" that is passed back from Christopher Robin to Pooh, Piglet, Kanga, and so forth until it reaches the untouch-able Alexander Beetle, the true order has already been more or less accurately restored. But it asserts itself most plainly in the fact that Pooh, by obeying his impulsive generosity and offering a stick to rescue Roo from the stream, has in fact discovered the North Pole. His official recognition as Discoverer of the Pole is only an outward, objective correlative for the inward purity of heart that justifies (in the eyes of the Milnean voice) his eminent position just below Christopher Robin in the Hierarchy.

We have, then, seen how Milne meant *Winnie-the-Pooh* to be read, and we can now appreciate the subtlety of technique that has beguiled three generations of fools into imagining that the book is nothing more than a group of children's stories. Indeed, the more we ponder *Pooh*'s complexity, the more we must wonder how any child could possibly enjoy these tales. Only a thorough versing in the Hierarchy of Heroism, combined with advanced training in the ironic reading of literary *personae* and a familiarity with multivalent symbolism, can prepare us adequately to approach the book. I have never met a child with any of these qualifications, much less with all three together. We cannot, after all, expect our children to see what the supposedly most competent critics of our time have failed to perceive. Now, however, we have succeeded in isolating the Milnean voice and the Christo-phoric ear; the underlying symbolic and dramaturgic principles of the book have been laid bare; and we may look forward to a day when all readers, from professors and parents to six-year-olds, will accept the Hierarchy of Heroism as naturally as they once accepted the super-ficially democratic comradeship of Christopher Robin and his rigidly classified row of underlings.

QUESTIONS AND STUDY PROJECTS

1. It is interesting to note how Window, in the classic manner of the careful scholar, is scrupulous to acknowledge his debts to the "pioneering works" of Poohology. Read the articles cited in Window's opening footnote, and write a paper in which you attempt to measure the depth of Window's gratitude to them.

2. Window distinguishes among four non-animal characters in *Pooh:* Milne, Christopher Robin, the Milnean voice, and the Christophoric ear. How many other such discriminations do you find it critically indispensable to make? Was Window justified, for example, in omitting the Christophoric voice and the Milnean ear?

MARTIN TEMPRALIS

wrote the following piece in 1939 for the New Reporter. *It is, as recent graduates of American high schools will recognize, an essay rather strictly governed by the application of a certain political dogma to literary questions. Your editor reprints it here (not without some misgivings) because it represents a particular style of criticism that was once in fashion. We live in a free society where virtually any opinion may be defended, including those of Mr. Tempralis in 1939. Your editor would like only to reassure all readers that he in no way subscribes to, supports, or, as it were, travels along with the views expressed in this essay. Naturally it is for each class, or rather for each student individually, freely to make up his own mind about the merit of Mr. Tempralis' argument. Teachers may, if they so choose, accompany this selection with an extra-credit, outside-reading assignment of Mr. J. Edgar Hoover's* Masters of Deceit.

Mr. Tempralis, formerly a New York journalist, returned to his native Jackson, Mississippi in 1946 and retired from the public eye for several years. He is now both publisher and editor of the Jackson White Democrat. *In 1956 he was commended by a Committee of the U. S. Senate for turning over his address book from the 1930's.*

A Bourgeois Writer's Proletarian Fables

MARTIN TEMPRALIS

> But who advances next, with cheerful grace,
> Joy in her eye, and plenty in her face?
> A wheaten garland does her head adorn:
> O Property! O goddess, English-born!
> —AMBROSE PHILLIPS (1714)

AFTER the sorry spectacle we have all enjoyed of England's desertion of Spain,[1] readers of this journal may well wonder why the further attention of serious persons should be wasted on British literature. I confess that this question has given me no little anguish of conscience; yet there are, upon consideration, reasons for persevering in our studies—provided, of course, that the

[1] This refers to political and military events which, having occurred some time ago and in a country that has remained quite untroubled ever since, need not be dwelt upon by the modern student.—Ed.

decadent *fin-de-siècle* doctrine of artistic "purity," of dis-
embodied literary thrills *à la* Walter Pater, is not allowed
to distract us from our goal. There remains, after all, the
good fight to wage; if one is sometimes forced to en-
vision the triumph of fascist Nazism not simply in Spain
but everywhere, such a prospect only strengthens one's
determination to strike a few more blows for the working
class before it is too late. We can remain serene in our
belief that, at least for those of us gifted with literary
sensibility, the struggle against Hitler can best be carried
on through pointing out the bourgeois-capitalistic elements in English literature. England remains today what
Marx originally derided it as being: that most bourgeois
of countries, characterized by a bourgeois aristocracy, a
bourgeois bourgeoisie, and a bourgeois proletariat. Under
these circumstances we need not despair of finding sufficient subject matter for our studies; and when we do run
across exceptional books or paragraphs that strike back
at the ruling class, we may also make use of these, exalting
them to the detriment and shame of other writers past
and present.

A. A. Milne, some might say, ought to deserve exemption from our interest, for he is chiefly known as the
author of innocuous prose and verse for small children.
I would reply that there are several heresies, distortions,
fallacies, and errors in that unconstructive attitude. Milne
has written plays and novels designed for grownups,
albeit bourgeois grownups. I confess that I have not read
this body of work, but a trustworthy friend has assured
me that it is more or less what one would have expected,
and hence proper material for criticism. The very idea
that any one writer should be deemed untouchable is, in
itself, rather too smacking of class privilege, and one is

not surprised to see that its proponents will not stand up to have themselves counted. Let us also be quite clear on the matter of children's literature. As the democratic experiments in group rearing have demonstrated in the Soviet Union, and as the sinister example of the *Deutsches Jungvolk* has admonished us in Germany, the period of childhood is the one in which lasting political impressions are conditioned into the individual. Literature is perhaps the foremost of all "educational" means, and the wide dissemination of Milne's four children's books justifies our concluding that he has had quite an impact on the thinking of the generation just now arriving at voting age. Will England turn even farther to the right, or will reason and progress begin to assert themselves? The only way to make an accurate prediction, I submit, is to analyze Milne's writings and bring to light their hidden socio-political implications.

Certainly there is nothing in Milne's background or reputation to encourage us toward optimism about his leanings. His origins were, I believe, thoroughly bourgeois, though I am not completely certain of this. I started reading his recently published *Autobiography* but was put off when I came across a reference to "our governess" on the third line of the first page. More to my taste—rather perverse in this case, I admit—is Milne's volume of pacifist sophistries, *Peace with Honour* (1934), in which he describes war in consummately funny English-bourgeois terms, utterly ignoring both the inevitability and the justice of proletarian revolution. War, says this comfortable Philistine, is "silly"; "This is not the way in which decent men and women behave"! How sweetly rational, how pious, and how abysmally ignorant of the economic facts of life this moralist must be! If my pass-

port had not been revoked I would travel across the
Atlantic just to meet such a perfect specimen of his type!

Let us not, however, dwell upon personalities, but
rather collect our literary evidence with dispassionate
objectivity. Our main interest will be the *Pooh* books,
though no student can afford to overlook the transpar-
ently revealing poems in *When We Were Very Young*
and *Now We Are Six*. All these works antedate Milne's
phase of loud revanchist pacifism (i.e. counterrevolution-
ism), yet all are undeniably "political" in import. A few
samples of poetry will suffice to introduce us to Milne's
general views. It is not an exaggeration to say that every
major social problem of industrial society is touched
upon, however callously and unintentionally, in these
"children's" rhymes. One hardly knows where to begin
the reckoning! Perhaps with "Disobedience," which be-
trays its promisingly Thoreauvian title by urging the
upper classes to "never go down to the end of the town"
where the working class lives? Perhaps with "Shoes and
Stockings," which cheerfully extols the labor of the many
for the few? Or with these charming lines from "King
Hilary and the Beggarman": *"Don't be afraid of doing
things. / (Especially, of course, for Kings.)"*? The field is
so rich that we may save valuable space here by simply
inviting the reader to browse through these volumes
himself, culling gems of imperialism, colonialism, and
profiteering.

Not astoundingly, the *Pooh* stories give us, at least at
first, the same distasteful impression as the poems. It is
hardly fortuitous that all the chief actors are property
owners with no apparent necessity to work; that they
are supplied as if by miracle with endless supplies of
honey, condensed milk, balloons, popguns, and extract

of malt; and that they crave meaningless aristocratic distinctions and will resort to any measure in their drive for class prestige. Not for nothing is the sycophant Pooh, eventually invested by Christopher Robin as "Sir Pooh de Bear, most faithful of all my Knights." It is a worthy ending to a series of tales in which every trace of social reality, every detail that might suggest some flaw in the capitalist paradise of pure inherited income, has been ruthlessly suppressed. Only, perhaps, in the ominous old sign beside Piglet's house do we glimpse the truth that this community of parasites is kept together through armed intimidation of the proletariat. "TRESPASSERS W," says the sign, and Piglet's facetious exegesis of this as his grandfather's name only reminds us more pointedly of the hereditary handing-on of the so-called sacred law of property.

This, then, is the literary world of *Winnie-the-Pooh*—an ideal ground, no doubt, for the darling offspring of the rich to develop their "insights" and "moral sense" upon! It would seem that no possible social good could come out of the extensive distribution of such books as these. And yet the scrupulous critic should hesitate before making such a sweeping condemnation. There is, perhaps, another light in which Milne's appallingly cheerful representation of *laissez-faire* life should be regarded. To borrow a leaf from our bourgeois rivals, the Freudian critics, we may say that the "unconscious" meaning of *Winnie-the-Pooh* seems quite opposite to its conscious, intended meaning. The very passages I have already cited could easily be interpreted in an ironical spirit, as subtle complaints against the abuses that seem to be extolled. I certainly do not mean to imply that the staunch "pacifist" A.A. Milne should receive any credit for this; it is rather a case of the social facts speaking for themselves in spite of all determined effort to deny their meaning. Milne is, after all, acknowledged by both "respectable" critics and by true lovers of literature to have hit upon some universal appeal in these stories. As there is only one kind of appeal that is truly universal (i.e. international), mere logic would lead us to believe that dialectical materialism, scientific socialism, the spirit of the Commune, democratic cooperation between peoples, and the necessity of revolution are implicitly urged upon us in Milne's stories. As indeed they are. Milne turns out to be a revolutionary *malgré lui*, an inspired simpleton who accepts the decadent state of his society with such naïve acquiescence that he unwittingly portrays its rottenness and points the way to its imminent overthrow.

The cynical reader may imagine that my argument has now become self-contradictory. What! Does *Winnie-the-Pooh* both suppress and reveal the social truth? Perhaps, dear reader, your doubts would have been expressed less smugly had you waited to hear my full explanation. Milne's stories *do* suppress the truth in refusing to represent the working class in its actual state of slavery to the bourgeoisie. The whole point of turning one's back on realism and retreating into animal fable—the effete tradition of Aesop and the royalist La Fontaine—is just to avoid facing the historical process whose end result has by now become evident to all. Yet this very literary subterfuge has undermined the author's purpose. As soon as Milne began seriously to treat his son's stuffed animals as living characters he apparently forgot to exercise his faculty of bourgeois censorship. In Pooh, Piglet, Eeyore, and the others we see *symbolically*, but with crystal clarity, an adumbration of the titanic struggle of rich and poor, oppressor and oppressed, that Milne and his "decent men and women" friends would fain have blotted from their consciousness!

All doubts about this "level of meaning" (as our effeminate aesthetes are fond of saying) in *Winnie-the-Pooh* may be removed at once if we consider the character of Rabbit, who is represented in such terms as these:

It was going to be one of Rabbit's busy days. As soon as he woke up he felt important, as if everything depended upon him. It was just the day for Organizing Something, or for Writing a Notice Signed Rabbit, or for Seeing What Everybody Else Thought About It. It was a perfect morning for hurrying round to Pooh, and saying, "Very well, then, I'll tell Piglet," and then going to Piglet, and saying, "Pooh thinks—but perhaps I'd better see Owl first." It was a Captainish sort of day, when everybody said, "Yes, Rabbit" and "No, Rabbit," and waited until he had told them.

Captainish indeed! Rabbit is the capitalist manager par excellence, the "captain of industry" who, though altogether a bungler and boaster, is bent upon imposing his will on everyone around him. Just the day for Writing a Notice Signed Rabbit! Here in a nutshell is a complete character study of the exploiter of labor, driven by a sense of shame at his exemption from toil to "busy" himself with writing bureaucratic and imperious notices, pretending that his arbitrary decisions have been democratically reached ("Pooh thinks—but perhaps I'd better see Owl first"), and demanding an automatic yes or no to each of his commands and rhetorical questions.

The interesting point, of course, is that this caricature of the bourgeois (if indeed it goes far enough to be called a caricature) is implicitly ridiculed by the plot of *Winnie-*

the-Pooh. I leave it to the squeaky-voiced "scholars" of our upper-class universities, clothed exquisitely in their flowing academic "gowns," to decide why the leisure-loving Milne arranged his book this way. The simple fact is that the net effect is proletarian. Try as he may to organize his acquaintances—that is, to keep them from organizing in self-protection against *him*—Rabbit never quite succeeds. On the very day mentioned above, for instance, he bustles vainly from Christopher Robin to Owl to Pooh to Piglet and Eeyore, failing in each case to drum up support for his schemes. These others employ the classic defenses of the disinherited proletariat when subjected to the high-sounding exhortations of their rulers: they either pretend to be elsewhere (Christopher

Robin), reply with courteous but meaningless ambiguity (Owl and Pooh), make themselves wholly inconspicuous (Piglet), or try to educate themselves to retort in kind (Eeyore). There is an atmosphere of buried sullenness, of potential revolt, in this chapter that is nothing short of inspiring. No less instructive is the story, "Pooh Goes Visiting," in which Rabbit, having deceitfully offered Pooh admittance to sample his overstocked larder, artfully traps his victim in the doorway and exploits him as an unsalaried towel rack for an entire week. As Shepard's illustration makes vivid for us, however, the united efforts of a Marxist-Leninist band of workers, constraining even the unwilling Rabbit to join in, succeed in extricating Pooh from his servitude.

Scarcely less central a symbolic character than Rabbit is Owl, the pedantic plutocrat who resides at "The Chestnuts, an old-world residence of great charm, which was grander than anybody else's." A spelling champion and a master of flowery, empty rhetoric, Owl is the necessary handservant to the raw acquisitive passion of Rabbit, which badly needs to be cloaked in grandiosities. The friendship of these two intellectual thugs is a perfect representation of the true role of "scholarship" in bourgeois-industrial society: the end purpose of Owl's obscure learning is to spread a veil of confusion over the doings of the fat cats, to cow the humble into submission before the graven idols of "objective truth" and "the Western tradition," and to rob the proletariat of its power to protest. What could be more meaningful than the fact that Owl has stolen the very tail from the back of Eeyore, the most downcast, bounced-upon member of society, and has converted it to his doorbell? When Pooh comes to retrieve it he is not so much as offered a lick of honey. Rabbit, the industrial manager, at least understood that one must give a subsistence in exchange for the worker's largely unpaid toil, but Owl, the "pure" scholar who professes to be innocent of the ways of the world, excuses himself from even this much elementary compassion. The *trahison des clercs* is the correct name for this sort of thing.

We should beware, however, of thinking that the

symbolic roles of Milne's characters remain absolutely static from one fable to the next. If the meaning is always essentially the same, the way of embodying it changes rather capriciously. Thus Pooh, who represents the workers' cause in the examples above, is cast as a wild-catting capitalist in the Heffalump chapter. He and Piglet, joint partners in the imperialistic venture of bringing back a live Heffalump (subjecting and exploiting colonial peoples), fall out over the question of who is to supply the capital (acorns or honey to set the trap) and who is to do the manual labor of pit-digging. The solution, naturally, is that the smaller and weaker Piglet is issued a shovel and put to work. Shepard's drawing of Piglet-as-miner, looking upward with mixed fatigue and resentment as the exacting supervisor Pooh arrives with the honey, is touching enough, one would think, to soften

the heart of a Father Coughlin or a Joseph Kennedy.[2] Pooh himself has been too loyal to his leisure-class environment (A. A. Milne's household) even to carry out the minimal duties of the capitalist properly: he has consumed most of the capital en route. Thus, of course, there ensues a general shortage of funds, which is still nothing in comparison with the hardship that will follow when it is discovered that Heffalumps do not even exist (i.e. that there never was a sufficient labor force in the subjected land to make the unnecessary product for the conspicuous consumption of an already bloated market). Pooh's nightmare of endless Heffalumps making straight for his honey supply and eating it all requires, I believe, no complicated analysis (and least of all a Freudian one!). It is the very image of proletarian revolution, of the workers arising in a concerted mass to seize the means of production from the jaded bourgeoisie.

One could go on incessantly with examples of this kind: Rabbit's racial prejudice against Kanga, Eeyore's housing problem and Pooh's misguided effort at slum clearance, Eeyore's own discrimination against Tigger and, reciprocally, Tigger's savage leaps against Eeyore, and so on. By now the reader will have got the message, and it is better not to drone on and on like our somber pundits in the "learned quarterlies," but to stop and hammer in the point once and for all. The world of *Pooh*, no less than that of the "idealistic" bourgeois pacifist Milne, is a world of sheer animalism, where the inhuman bestiality of the "free" market has full sway. In this unconsciously revealing portrait of capitalism we glimpse, not only the sordidness of wage-slavery, speculation, and "lawful" gangsterism, but also the possibility of a better life—of a

2 A religious and a political figure, respectively.—Ed.

forthcoming heroic revolution of oppressed peoples establishing free democratic socialist communes of brotherly peace-loving workers who will march side by side down the collective road to prosperity and equality for all. This optimistic note, which is in fact the ultimate meaning of *Winnie-the-Pooh*, is what rescues the book from the vilest decadence and makes it, after all, suitable reading for progressive children throughout the world.

QUESTIONS AND STUDY PROJECTS

1. In our Freshman English courses we try to show that everyone, within certain very broad limits, is entitled to his opinion on any subject. Do you feel that Tempralis was entitled to his 1939 opinions about *Pooh?* Why not?

2. Tempralis seems obsessed with "fascism," doesn't he? Look up this difficult word in your dictionary and explain its meaning to the class.

P[AUL] R[AYMOND] HONEYCOMB

was born and raised in Brookline, Massachusetts, but now regards himself as a "fragmented, twisted" citizen of Rome, Tokyo, and London. The merit of his verse, long known to readers of the "little magazines," has now been acknowledged by a broader public, while his elegant, intensely personal criticism, tending in recent years to be mixed with incisive travel notes, has always been admired. Although he never bothered to complete his formal education, Mr. Honeycomb has in recent years found a residence at Cornell, where, he says, "one issues Orphic utterings for the grads to furrow their fronts over." He recalls with some pride that he was the one to discover Wallace Stevens, or that Wallace Stevens was the one to discover him. He cannot quite remember which it was, but in either case, he says, "the possibilities are fructifying."

The Theory and Practice of Bardic Verse: Notations on the Hums of Pooh

P. R. HONEYCOMB

ALMOST, one does not know where to begin. This Pooh, excruciated by ponderings as to the whatness and the howness of things, can startle by the windings

and rewindings of his imagination, by murky gyrations wherein we can scarcely follow. Pick a hum at random. Start, let us say for sheer cussedness, with the first one:

It's a very funny thought that, if Bears were Bees,
They'd build their nests at the bottom of trees.

And that being so (if the Bees were Bears),
We shouldn't have to climb up all these stairs.

Here is thought seeming to strike us in its amoebic forth-rightness, thought not teased nearly out of rhyme but flowing, flowed by furry teddy-bear motives into the form and substance of desire. Desire I say, for Pooh wants merely to find a path topwards to the tree's honey-prize; but desire has its own adamantine logic, the logic of desperate interchange: if Bears were Bees.

Whimsy, too. Look again at the lines of verse that have somehow managed to inhabit our first paragraph (mys-teriously, perhaps prophetically, they have taken up resi-dence there). The faint jarring of *vraisemblance* that reaches us in bears building nests swells portentously into the *buffo*, as the ascent, the surmounting of a tree renders itself in terms of climbing stairs. It is the bear-imagina-tion, to say nothing for the moment of the teddy-bear imagination, that ursifies the bee psychology, while through it all the re-anthropomorphization of Christo-pher's and Milne's man-imagination asserts itself in the final, deceptively meek monosyllable, "stairs." If Bees were Bears.

This then, as Ramón Fernandez used to say, is poetry. Poetry, surely, impressing us little with the taint of art, much less with the pinker taint of artiness, but nonethe-less artful, pure and powerful as Beefeater gin, a sock in the eye delivered with finesse and musculature. Yet Pooh is elusive, double, profoundly not there when you think he is.

On Thursday, when it starts to freeze
And hoar-frost twinkles on the trees,
How very readily one sees
That these are whose—but whose are these?

We think first, of course, of Shakespeare and his icicles by the wall, the enforced simplicity of the citified rustic now playing rustic for the city, rejoicing mock-innocently in freezing milk and runny noses. Pooh, though, adds the problematic, the tormented: *but whose are these?* "How very readily one sees" Colin Clout metamorphosed into Joseph K. in these lines; how André Gide waits, all patiently, to inherit the condemned playground when the last snowball has been airily tossed.

Shakespeare as Bard. Bardic verse, the bear as bard: the topic that has thrust itself upon these meditations, bringing order where there was none before. Pooh brings us, still in his capacity as snow-singer I mean, a Nordic sense of the vital elements that must wiggle into asseveration on their own terms: no hothouse stuff. "But it's no good going home to practise it, because it's a special Outdoor Song which Has To Be Sung In The Snow." The firmness of the Icelandic *scop* in London, 1926! Of course it can only be embodied, made flesh, in teddy-bear flesh. This London belongs to Eliot and his falling towers, to false teeth and the gramophone; if we are to have our bard we must find him in the nursery, not even in the child (for the child too, already, has trundled through the fog to lay himself at the feet of Mickey Mouse and Superman, or their twenty-sixish equivalents), but in the child's one possible, impossible hope of what a very perfect bear could be like:

Not as a god, but as a god might be.

That, of course, is not Christopher Robin speaking but Stevens—the presence, at least for me, behind much of these cerebral goings-on in the creative consciencing of Pooh. I thought of Stevens just yesterday in Yucatán. I

was there for Uncle Sam, ostensibly telling them about
W. S. Merwin but really checking up on the Alliance
for Progress, which all the local poets told me is a wash-
out. The sun was red just over the jungle, a dark girl
with big hips and a raw, female smell handed me a tequila,
and I thought of Stevens with his passion for the sensual,
chthonic South.

> *This warm and sunny Spot*
> *Belongs to Pooh.*

There is a difference here, unmistakable, not residual,
from Stevens' luxuriant, faintly rotting bask in Caribbean
heat; also from Crane:

> *In these poinsettia meadows of her tides,*
> *Adagios of islands, O my Prodigal,*
> *Complete the dark confessions her veins spell.*

Nothing dirty like this going on in Pooh; nothing, any-
way, that writhes surfaceward sufficiently for us to savor
its incantation. Always and ever, instead, Pooh sends
forth emanations of the pure infantile greed that we
welcome and forgive, it so cheers us for our own grayer,
wryer wants. Childhood is a warm and sunny spot we
gladly cede for the privilege of seeing it occupied again.
As for ourselves, there is turning and turning but no re-
turning, the heart's decimations are always there ready
to snarl us back to the purgatory of our majority. (I
think of Dante as I write these lines; I wonder what
Dante would have thought of them if he could have read
them. Possibly not much, his mind was so ineluctably
other.)

I was speaking, I believe, of Stevens, whose very insurance policies breathed the unfettered leewardings off

Key West that so possessed him. And Crane too, although of course the point about insurance doesn't hold in his case; indeed he was rather a bad risk. I think I was telling myself that Pooh's sun is alien from that of these two American fabulators; and it is. But one feels, almost, the strong moist necessity to put in a word for similarities. Stevens and his mythy kingdoms of mind, Pooh and his mystical Forest of childhood: "the Forest will always be there . . . and anybody who is Friendly with Bears can find it." Milne speaking, of course, announcing a surreptitious Poetic, a defense of poesy as ever-regenerative, the only time-machine we have. And later, Pooh himself puts in an ontological word. Piglet has doubted whether Pooh's Ode to him, which at first sight looks as pure and false as Pindar upon whose locker-room eulogies it is patently modeled, really has told the truth.

"Did I really do all that?" he said at last.
"Well," said Pooh, "in poetry—in a piece of poetry—well, you *did* it, Piglet, because the poetry says you did. And that's how people know."

False, you see, but not naïve, and not false in Pindar's sense of toadying to the fixed system of glory, either. Pooh sees what Stevens retold us in endless formulations, that truth is what the mind creates for itself. Since the imperfect is so hot in us, we must use flawed words to hedge us round with our own reality, to sing beyond the genius of the sea and so become the very music that we sing. All this has been commonplace now for several years. What we are just beginning to understand is that Pooh's hums, no less than "The Blue Guitar," belong too in this epistemological haven of rival creation, this mythopoeia that has gone beyond Pyrrhonism.

Further hums, further determinations.

> *They all went off to discover the Pole,*
> *Owl and Piglet and Rabbit and all;*
> *It's a Thing you Discover, as I've been tole*
> *By Owl and Piglet and Rabbit and all.*
> *Eeyore, Christopher Robin and Pooh*
> *And Rabbit's relations all went too—*
> *And where the Pole was none of them knew. . . .*
> *Sing Hey! for Owl and Rabbit and all!*

Contemplating these lines, which I have copied down laboriously from the text, I seem to see an inner purposiveness in the title for this article, which I had simply placed at the top of a blank sheet, my *Pooh* opened hopefully before me. Bardic verse: the American Bard of them all, lying even all improbably behind Stevens with his double indemnities and limits of liability. Whitman of course; for the hum in question was composed *during* the Expotition, problematically, unwindingly, like *Leaves of Grass.* Pooh too is hoping to cease not until death, sounding his barbaric yawp over the roofs of the world as he saunters out for the Pole, the *Ultima Thule* of the fancy. Of course this poem, as the Second Law of Thermodynamics teaches us, must run down eventually, but this is said by common sense intruding with its nasty big brother reason to spoil the spirit's party, and we needn't allow it. We can think of Pooh like Whitman going on endlessly, not even sinking into a rocker in Camden, New Jersey, but just ever articulating his daydreams, compacting the diaphanous wisps of his imaginings into verse. And where the Pole was none of them knew, nor really hoped to discover. Each of us dies, as Gatsby learned, when the green light is attained and examined.

This Whitman thing, there is no getting round it. The

hums of Pooh are a great analogic body to *Leaves of Grass*. Thematically what is there to choose between the two? How is the mystical Forest of childhood different from Walt's fantasy of going to live with the cows, of throwing off guilt and respectability for a live relation to the blood's flushing madness? And methodology, which really appears to be becoming our theme as this essay strives more archingly toward organicity: methodologically, Pooh is such another Whitman that he might well fear Whitman's ghostly reappearance, Jolly Corner-style. Listen to Pooh composing; he has just gotten as far as *"Sing Ho! for the life of a Bear"*:

When he had got as far as this, he stretched his head, and thought to himself "That's a very good start for a song, but what about the second line?" He tried singing "Ho," two or three times, but it didn't seem to help. "Perhaps it would be better," he thought, "if I sang Hi for the Life of a Bear." So he sang it . . . but it wasn't. "Very well, then," he said, "I shall sing that first line twice, and perhaps if I sing it very quickly, I shall find myself singing the third and fourth lines before I have time to think of them, and that will be a Good Song. Now then . . ."

He tries it, and it works. Almost, one might say, this passage epitomizes the two rival Poetics of our whole tradition. There is the meticulous, thoughtful, conscious style of Horace and Pope, the eternal faith in revision and self-analysis; and there's the quick, sub-rational, heart-and-liver thudding faith of Shelley and Whitman, which Pooh takes up in his second try. It is all stated more simply later, when Piglet has objected to "pounds, *shillings*, and ounces" as units of weight. The shillings, says Pooh, "wanted to come in after the pounds, . . . so

I let them. It is the best way to write poetry, letting things come." This is surely the very trick and note of Whitman's careless pyrotechnics, as both his well-wishers and detractors quasi-chorically agree.

In wondering what I shall set down next in these notations, I am reminded of Heisenberg's Uncertainty Principle. The only thing that is certain is that I am uncertain what to set down next, and in this I typify the whole modern age and the collision of elementary particles in particular, a fact I find peculiarly comforting. Just lately a publisher sent me—for I am on everyone's complimentary copy list, don't ask me how I managed it—a book on game theory and probability. I know less than nothing about this, but it struck me at once as both relevant and irrelevant to poetry, which, though of all games the most improbable, makes its improbabilities fixed and irrevocable as Monday morning. One thinks of Pooh and his seeming meanders that are in reality purposeful circles:

> It's very, very funny,
> 'Cos I know I had some honey;
> 'Cos it had a label on,
>   Saying HUNNY.

> A goloptious full-up pot too,
> And I don't know where it's got to,
> No, I don't know where it's gone—
>   Well, it's funny.

The childish handling of connectives here, giving us deceitfully a feeling of breathless consecutiveness, masks the cunning circumferentiality of the piece. Pooh's italicized *know* strives recklessly against the inbounding of his world, while the inexorable ·structure of his verse works onward to the final repetition of "funny," dropping us and Pooh precisely where we were initially, only now supped-full with horrors: with the trembling conviction that, as Heisenberg might have put it, you can't really know where your honey pot has got to; it is molecularly out of the question. Thus Pooh joins Pirandello and the others, the dissociated moderns with whom he is in such good company.

It is this modernicity in Pooh that enables us to forgive his occasional peccadilloes; for it is true that in his deep viscous confusions, his sophistications of heuristic regression, Pooh sometimes sins against art. His coinages are not always of the most persuasive:

> And a sort of sqoze
> Which grows and grows
> Is not too nice for his poor old nose,
> And a sort of squch
> Is much too much
> For his neck and his mouth and his ears and such.

Nor, in all straightforwardness, can we quite absolve him from the charge of a trace of padding here and there:

> I don't much mind if it rains or snows,
> 'Cos I've got a lot of honey on my nice new nose,
> I don't much care if it snows or thaws,
> 'Cos I've got a lot of honey on my nice clean paws!

The sense in which Pooh's nose is new and paws are clean has thus far escaped me, and I fear the worst, I fear that the operation of intelligence has been blurred by the nagging exigencies of meter. But with Pooh one never knows. There is always the purple possibility, the dancing chance, that meaning has seeped over, honeylike, into these apparently lesser relations of the strong words in the hum. In Pooh there is always the need, felt maddeningly as implacable by virtue of the singer's very simplicity, to cry up, cry down, cry in or cry out, the over-full poignancies of man's or bear's fate, of the numbing torments of the victim whose sufferings are such that no regular metaphysic, no grammar of regular form, can body them forth. Behind the lisping numbers of childhood we hear the deracinated howl of the soul's quick, and this, as I say, comforts us, for it convinces us that Pooh is if anything a modern, one of us, and therefore ultimately worthy in spite of all, if not indeed because of all.

QUESTIONS AND STUDY PROJECTS

1. Elsewhere Honeycomb has defined poetry as "reason reservedly yawning its great unseasonable limits beyond the solipsistic; self-masticating music; flawed felony of feeling snatched from the universal slagheap of the particular." Discuss.

2. It is plain from Honeycomb's essay that modern man is dissociated and alienated, isn't it? You, as a young modern man or woman, form a part of this piecemeal world that is mirrored in Kafka, Pirandello, and *Pooh*. Try to think of the most "fragmented" or "rootless" thing that has happened to you—perhaps an incident during one of your summer vacations from high school—and write a paper around it, showing yourself to be a qualified modern.

MYRON MASTERSON,

though born and raised in Queens, describes himself as "a native son of the Old West—the genuine Old West." By this he probably means the Colorado School of Mines, where he is the mainstay of the English Department when not traveling. A regular contributor to Commentary *and the* Partisan Review, *Mr. Masterson has been known as a distinguished American "angry young man" for the past twenty years. The present article resulted from a series of lectures at the American University at Beirut, where Mr. Masterson was passing one of his not infrequent Fulbright Professorships in 1953.*

Poisoned Paradise:
The Underside of *Pooh*

MYRON MASTERSON

BEFORE going further I would like to thank all the people who have made this article possible: Karl Marx, St. John of the Cross, Friedrich Nietzsche, Sacco and Vanzetti, Sigmund Freud, and C. G. Jung. Some finicky "experts" have said that there exist differences of opinion among these thinkers. The point, however, is that each of them has helped to shape my literary and moral consciousness; and that, frankly, is enough for me. If the reader is surprised by the eclecticism with which I draw inspiration from a free-wheeling, broad-minded range of sources, that is his problem and not mine.

Perhaps one more private note would not be out of place in this otherwise impersonal analysis. I first discovered the real meaning of *Winnie-the-Pooh* when I was reading selections from *When We Were Very Young* to my twelve children. Suddenly my youngest son, Charlie, stopped me and asked to hear these lines from "The Mirror" again:

> *And there I saw a white swan make*
> *Another white swan in the lake.*

"God, how did they let that one get through?" lisped Trudy. And little Steven said, "That's nothing. Read that real wild couplet from 'Vespers.'" With mingled misgiving and interest I allowed Billy and Jane to fumble their tiny fingers through the pages until they came upon these lines, which were recited in gleeful unison:

> God bless Mummy. *I know that's right.*
> *Wasn't it fun in the bath tonight?*

Wisdom from the mouths of babes! A rapid check of the other poems in the volume, and then a similar run-through of *Now We Are Six*, convinced me that all Milne's verse was more or less equally salacious. With the zeal of Dick Tracy I turned to the *Pooh* books to extend my discovery. The result, printed below for the first time, has shocked and enraged Philistine audiences from Tokyo to Wauwatosa, Wisconsin, and I am thinking of working it up into a monograph.

To clear the air a bit, let us reach an understanding about the alleged "purity" of children's literature in general. There was a period when I felt it necessary to cancel one title after another from the "approved" list in our family bedtime reading. I don't regard myself as an arch-conservative, but the atmosphere of polymorphous perverse play in *Little Women* was too much for me; while the uterine fantasies in *Alice in Wonderland* have been known to scholarship for years. One volume after another had to be transferred from the toddlers' shelf to my own locked bookcase—*Uncle Wiggly* (!), *The Arabian Nights*, *The Tale of Mrs. Tittlemouse*—until one day I realized that soon there would be nothing left! I was forced to reconsider the entire question of Repugnancy in Literature. After a good deal of soul-searching I came up with this answer: All children's books, like all other books, are knit together by archetypal patterns emanating from the collective unconscious of the race. Children, being essentially people, are likewise shot through with archetypes; hence the appeal of children's literature to them. The difference between *Peter Rabbit* and *Peyton Place* is not that one is pure and the other impure, but that the archetypes are disguised in one case and fairly obvious in the other. Since the communication of archetypes occurs largely in the unconscious, the average child never knows, as it were, what is hitting him. And thus we can go back to the nursery with a clear conscience and an armload of restored classics. The special insight shown by my own children—Susie, Henry, Jane, and the rest—should be attributed to the fact that they have attended many of my public lectures.

Ignoring, then, the superficial level of *Winnie-the-Pooh*, let us dive at once, like Melville's Catskill eagle, into the profundities and sub-profundities of the matter. It is not hard to dismiss the generally accepted impression of this book as a cheery, chins-up collection of anecdotes designed to educate Christopher Robin in the gentle virtues of English social life. Milne's chief spokesman, Eeyore, is a veritable Thersites, a malcontent who would have put Marston to shame. No pretense of "helpfulness" or "conviviality" escapes his wickedly incisive rebuttal. Nor, when we look around at the other characters, do we find a much rosier picture. The "lovable" Pooh is tragically fixated at the narcissistic stage of development.[1] Rabbit and Owl are aging bachelors whose respective megalomania and fussiness are tempered only by their mutual friendship, of which the less said, the better. Kanga is the archetypal mawkish "Mom"-figure we see exemplified everywhere in America. And Piglet, Tigger, and Roo are such advanced cases that their problems must be analyzed separately below. As for Christopher Robin, his interest in these toy animals is undoubtelly "normal," if by normality we understand a neurotic effort to transfer onto one's furry dolls all the grievances and secret fantasies that characterize the onset of the latency period. "Aye, madam, it is common," as Hamlet remarked to his mother—but it isn't pretty!

The fact, indeed, that Christopher Robin has recently suffered the destruction and repression of his Oedipus Complex provides a key to the whole tone, as well as to many of the incidents, in *Winnie-the-Pooh*. The phase Christopher is entering is that of maximum repression, when toys, hobbies, games, and schoolwork hopefully will receive the libido that was previously lavished upon thoughts of "Mummy." Even in the most successful cases, however, the repression is incomplete; we can always see, if we try, a survival of the old incestuous wishes and a rather suspiciously overeager attempt to desexualize oneself and one's imaginary companions. Not without significance does Milne, who must be only too happy to see his little boy finally turning his conscious thoughts elsewhere, dedicate the book "To Her"—the mother who

[1] " 'Oh, Bear!' said Christopher Robin. 'How I do love you!' 'So do I,' said Pooh.' "

never appears *in propria persona*, but who lurks behind every page as the not-quite-relinquished goal, the secretly intended object of all Christopher Robin's "portentous little activity" (to quote *The Turn of the Screw*).[2] The animals in *Winnie-the-Pooh* are lacking in genitalia, they seem to have no other activity in life beyond calling on one another and eating snacks—but the experienced critic need not be fooled. The real subject of the book is Christopher Robin's loss of his mother, which is alternately symbolized, accepted, protested against, denied, and homoerotically compensated for in the various "nursery" stories of the plot.

From the portrait of Christopher Robin himself, of course, we should expect the least enlightenment, since it is upon his toy animals that he attempts to project his forbidden fantasies. It is clear to the reader that Christopher knows what is off limits once one has entered the latency period in earnest.[3] More revealing is the almost total absence of parents for the other characters in the story. Whenever Pooh and Piglet imagine that they are in danger they wish to be soothed, not by their own fathers and mothers, but by Christopher Robin; and the same holds true for the other animals. Surely this can-

2 After I gave this lecture at Majorca last year, Robert Graves told me that in his opinion "Her" meant the White Goddess, the Belle Dame Sans Merci of whom Graves has written so very, very often. This is entirely possible, and the reader may entertain both Graves's idea and mine at once, only remembering that mine came first.

3 See, e.g., the way he shies away from the subject of phallic "Poles," of which he professes to be ignorant because "people don't like talking about them." Pooh, on the contrary, wants to go at once in search of the East Pole, "but Christopher Robin had thought of something else to do with Kanga." This last clause may imply a return of the repressed; note the vague intentions regarding the mother-surrogate Kanga.

not be explained by saying that these dolls weren't *any-one's* children. *Winnie-the-Pooh* is virtually haunted by ancestral figures: Piglet's grandfather Trespassers William, Owl's revered Uncle Robert, Pooh's mysterious forebear Mr. Sanders, and so on. The amazing fact is that there is no shortage of distant and dead relations but a severe want of immediate ones on the scene. And the point of it all is indisputable: Christopher Robin, still smarting under the paternal castration threat and the enforced renunciation of the mother, has decreed a ban on mothers and fathers in general. He has imagined for himself a blissful teddy-bearland in which no adult is permitted to intrude. He himself will be the sole father figure, and will "show up" his own severe parents by exercising only a gentle brotherly supervision of his charges.

Here, then, we have the rationale of the ideal world that Christopher Robin has hallucinated—a pastoral paradise, a garden of fun in which the danger of incest and punishment is nil. But like all such gardens, as Hawthorne was I believe the first to notice, something is likely to go awry sooner or later. In this case it is the entrance of Kanga that transforms *Winnie-the-Pooh*, with one brutal stroke, from the genre of bucolic idyll to that of depth-psychological Gothic tale of terror. The true meaning of Kanga's arrival—the installation of the emasculating Female as overseer of the doomed frolickers—is not lost on Rabbit, who does everything in his power to exclude her. All in vain! From the very moment of Kanga's appearance the pastoral playground is overshadowed by doubt and guilt, for the all-too-loving *anima*-Woman has pitched her temple here!

We should pay special attention to the fact that Baby Roo forms part of this invasion, for it is *as Roo's mother* that Kanga threatens the common happiness. All Christopher Robin's animals had, by his fiat, entered a kind of latency period of their own, never bothering themselves over the fundamental questions that small children want to ask their parents. Now Enter Kanga:

Nobody seemed to know where they came from, but there they were in the Forest: Kanga and Baby Roo. When Pooh asked Christopher Robin, "How did they come here?" Christopher Robin said, "In the Usual Way, if you know what I mean, Pooh," and Pooh, who didn't, said "Oh!" Then he nodded his head twice and said, "In the Usual Way. Ah!"

No one, I think, will deny that these lines deal with the topic, "Where do babies come from?" No one can fail to draw the inference that Christopher Robin feels basically evasive on this subject; and no one will forget that this is entirely in keeping with my understanding of Kanga's role. The verification of my inspired guesswork, I confess, strengthens my resolution never to read the criticism of others but merely to rely on placing my unconscious in sympathetic rapport with that of the writer.

Kanga's corrosive effect on Christopher Robin's ideal society, like Margaret Fuller's on Brook Farm, stems from her desire to bring every male under her sway. I need hardly dwell on her treatment of Roo ("Later, Roo dear," "We'll see, Roo dear"); it is enough to make us all breathe a sigh of relief at having successfully crossed the border of puberty. More interesting thematically is her capture of Piglet. Piglet is, we may say, the very archetype of the sickly, nervous little boy who is terrified by father and mother alike.[4] His fear of emasculation and his horror

4 Don't get me wrong; Piglet's actual father doesn't appear in the flesh. He comes in his essential traumatic form as angry castrator. See Piglet's nightmare in which he is chased by the grossly phallic Heffalump, and in which he hopes desperately for protection

of intercourse converge in his abject quaking before the pit for Heffalumps, the "Cunning Trap" as he slyly calls it. He and King Lear agree entirely about this "sulphurous pit." And his misgivings turn out to have been all too justified. Piglet becomes Kanga's very first victim outside her immediate family. Instead of helping in the plan to blackmail Kanga into leaving, he finds himself stuffed into her womblike pouch, vigorously bathed and rubbed, and nearly made to swallow Roo's fulsome baby medicine. Ugh! It is a section of the book that I can scarcely stand to reread! Piglet's symbolic spaying is complete when Kanga, continuing the pretense that she is serving Roo, explains that the medicine is "to make you grow big and strong, dear. You don't want to grow up small and weak like Piglet, do you? Well, then!" From this moment onward Piglet, who certainly never showed much virility before, is fit only to try out for countertenor in a choir.[5]

Kanga's role is raised to positively allegorical dimensions when she encounters Tigger in *The House at Pooh Corner*. Tigger is the one "intruder" in that volume, as Kanga and Roo were in the previous one, and this fact alone shows us how gutless the Pooh-world has become in the interim under Kanga's influence. For Tigger, the embodiment of pure Dionysiac energy, of sheer animal potency, appears strange and unwelcome to this melancholy band of castrati.[6] Alas, poor Tigger! Nothing in

---

from his grandfather—a typical childish recourse in such cases, by the way.

5 Note also the irony that Piglet is trapped and degraded by Kanga as a result of his expectation that *he* would trap *her*. How frighteningly womanly that is!

6 Bear in mind that Tigger arrives *without a family*, indeed without any real certainty that there exist others of his species.

the Forest is fit for him to eat but Roo's extract of malt, which must be administered by Kanga. And could we reasonably expect this matriarch to stand by idly and watch her household being overrun with sheer maleness? She sinks her hooks into Tigger at once:

"Well, look in my cupboard, Tigger dear, and see what you'd like." Because she knew at once that, however big Tigger seemed to be, he wanted as much kindness as Roo.

As much kindness as Roo, forsooth! This is the beginning of the end. Sinclair Lewis, Wright Morris, and Evan S. Connell, Jr., all working together, could never nauseate us half so successfully as does the picture of Kanga waving good-by to Roo and Tigger as they take their watercress and extract-of-malt sandwiches off for a sexless *déjeuner sur l'herbe.*

It is when things have reached this sorry pass that the inevitable homoerotic alternative to compulsory innocence suddenly offers itself to Kanga's victims. Already in *Winnie-the-Pooh* Piglet had reached a point comparable

---

Like modern America, the Pooh-world is one in which a Whole Man must find himself alone, resented, and misunderstood.

to Huckleberry Finn's satanic resolution to prefer hellfire to the female-dominated world he has thus far inhabited.[7] Now, in the excitement over getting Tigger and Roo down from a heavily symbolic tree, Piglet flips:

> But Piglet wasn't listening, he was so agog at the thought of seeing Christopher Robin's blue braces again. He had only seen them once more, when he was much younger, and, being a little over-excited by them, had had to go to bed half an hour earlier than usual . . .

Christopher Robin is flattered and attracted by this fetishistic response to his little striptease, but he is naturally reluctant to enter into serious relations with a pig. Doubtless he has designs on one of the tiny scholars with whom he is now learning spelling and mathematics. Piglet, therefore, is thrown into the willing arms of Pooh, who at the end of the book welcomes him into his house as permanent roommate. Nor should we omit Tigger and Roo from this account. What, after all, did Roo have in mind ascending that tree on Tigger's back, squeaking "Oo, Tigger—oo, Tigger—oo, Tigger"? What is the meaning of Tigger's compulsion to "bounce" upon all his male friends? Roo, at least, gets the point even if innocent readers have not done so: "Try bouncing *me*, Tigger," he passionately pleads.

Well then! This, within the limits of my volatile, intuitive temperament, is a sober and accurate account of *Winnie-the-Pooh*'s meaning. Were I to read other critics I would be sure to find that my interpretation has con-

7 "At first he thought that the whole world had blown up; and then he thought that perhaps only the Forest part of it had; and then he thought that perhaps only *he* had, and he was now alone in the moon or somewhere, and would never see Christopher Robin or Pooh or Eeyore again. And then he thought, 'Well, even if I'm in the moon, I needn't be face downwards all the time . . .'"

tradicted every threadbare cliché on the subject. I am sincerely sorry if this article must spread consternation in the ranks of four-eyed old professors and mooning Moms. But the truth, after all, must be told by someone; someone must bear the burden of demonstrating that English literature, since Shakespeare's day, has demoted itself continually from maturity down through pimply post-pubescence to the nervous sublimations of the latency period, and now stands on the brink of re-entry through the Oedipus and castration complexes. It is a fascinating, rewarding process to watch—particularly for myself, a simple, milk-fed boy of the Mesas, just glad to be a vigorous American critic in the middle of the twentieth century!

QUESTIONS AND STUDY PROJECTS

1. Of the various authorities whom Masterson acknowledges as his literary and moral guides, which do you think influenced him the most? Perhaps one member of your class could look into St. John of the Cross, another Sacco and Vanzetti, and so on. There may be a joint term-paper project here!

2. Masterson's conclusions are bound to arouse some disagreement, but we can all grant his point that Kanga is a "Mom" figure, as he puts it. Write an essay on the importance of the American Mother in the home, in the community and nation, and on the international scene today.

C[YRUS] J[ACKSON] L[EE] CULPEPPER

was born in Baton Rouge and educated at Chapel Hill and Oxford. Although he is presently teaching at Southern Methodist, he wants your editor to assure his readers that he is "not of the Dissenting persuasion." He has published significant articles on the Essay on Man, Wordsworth's White Doe of Rylestone, *and the works of Ivy Compton-Burnett, "placing them all," as he says, "within the roomy fabric of the Christian-Humanist tradition." Presently he is at work on a monograph proving that Shakespeare was familiar with the teachings of the Essene Sect and that his plays must be reinterpreted accordingly.*

O Felix Culpa!
The Sacramental Meaning of
Winnie-the-Pooh

C. J. L. CULPEPPER, D.Litt., Oxon.

THE miniscule handful of persons already acquainted with my studies in English literature will recognize by my present title that a new, and perhaps not insignificant, effort is being made here: namely, to find within a children's story the components of genuine art. By "art" I of course understand the *dulcis et utile* canon familiar to classical, medieval, and renaissance writers alike—with a good deal greater emphasis on the *utile*, to be sure. When Homer saw to it that the impious Hector was dragged around the walls of Troy three times, he was teaching a lesson about the triple pitfalls of Pride. When Tamburlaine was permitted to sack cities and sink himself in every luxurious vice, the saintly Marlowe was (as Roy Battenhouse has shown us) pointing a moral about the impermanence of the flesh. In every case of authentic

literature—and the reader will be able to supply innumerable examples from his own experience—the literary
value results from a kernel of serious moral doctrine that
is surrounded by a superficial appeal to the eye and ear.
The business of criticism, as I comprehend it, is to peel
away this outer husk, discard it where it will do no further
harm, and expose the core of *sententia* for all to understand. The responsibility I am currently imposing upon
my modest analytic powers is that of finding this central
meaning in *Winnie-the-Pooh*.

It comes as no surprise, I feel sure, to most readers
when they are told that this charming little volume contains exhortations to virtue. The hasty view of Robertus
Tracy, that from *Winnie-the-Pooh* "*Educatio ethica
clementer abest*," [1] cannot be generally shared. It may
well be doubted whether any children's literature, much
less a book that has proven its durability so convincingly
as this one, is lacking in instruction. What remains at
issue, however, is the far more interesting question
whether the moral teaching is of a Christian or merely a
generally "moralistic" nature, as is unfortunately the case
in most such stories. It is all very well for little red
engines to huff and puff up steep gradients to illustrate
the necessity of Trying Harder, but this doesn't bring us
any closer to salvation, does it? The *Iliad*, in contrast,
though its author labored under the inconvenience of a
painful anachronism, points us heavenward as surely as
does the wand of Mercury in Botticelli's "Primavera."
The task before us is therefore clear: first, to certify
Winnie-the-Pooh as legitimate literature by demonstrating that it contains Christian dogma; and secondly, to

1 Robertus Tracy, "Ursus Minor, or, The Bear as Swain," *Carleton Miscellany*, II (Summer, 1961), 118.

raise it to the level of *great* literature by showing the historic purity of its connection to the traditional sources of Christian thought, in opposition to the erroneous whimsies of Latitudinarians and Enthusiasts.[2]

Let me proclaim at once that, although there are few overt citations of Holy Writ in *Winnie-the-Pooh*, the subject of the book is nothing other than the central drama of our faith: the Fall and Redemption of Man. We Christian critics learned long ago not to be put off by a secular or even an impious tone in literary works. If one is convinced that a particular book contains greatness, and if that book persists in refusing to come out forthrightly and preach to us, the only answer must be that its dogma is communicated allegorically. This, by the way, was exactly St. Augustine's principle in recommending the study of the ancient classics, and gentle Chaucer expressed the same sentiment: "al that writen is/ To oure doctrine it is y-write, y-wis." When we return to *Winnie-the-Pooh* with the exemplary tradition of Spenser, Bunyan, and Milton in mind, we perceive without difficulty not one allegorical plot, but many—and all tending, I need hardly say, to the moral education of the Christian gentleman, the very purpose that guided Spenser unflaggingly through 3,850 thrilling stanzas of the *Faerie Queene*.[3]

To begin at the beginning, the reader is invited to peer more closely than is his wont at the opening chapter of *Winnie-the-Pooh*. What does he find? A story about a

2 I cannot recall, at the moment, the name of the English novelist who described Sophocles as a kind of Anglican Bishop before his time; but the similitude is just, and expresses the measure of that dramaturgist's enduring appeal.

3 Which was left tragically incomplete about halfway through the author's original plan.—Ed.

certain tree which proves irresistibly attractive to our hero, who conceives a passion for removing and eating something he finds upon it. With increasing pride in his ability to snatch the spoils without assistance, much less with official permission to touch this certain product, he climbs nearly to the top of the tree and—*falls!* (Italics mine.) Moreover, once the *lapsus* has been acted through, it must of course repeat itself endlessly, at least until the Atonement comes. Thus Pooh, the Adam-substitute, hav-

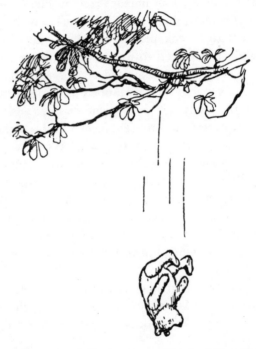

ing landed sorrowfully in a gorse-bush (East of Eden), betakes himself directly back to the forbidden food with renewed lust. This time he is significantly black from head to toe, and is pursued and tormented by *"the wrong sort of bees*" (italics Pooh's), little avengers which, in bringing to my mind both Christian devils and the Eumenides of Aeschylus, provide a perfect illustration of that marriage of pagan and holy which we call by the name of Christian Humanism.[4]

This simple example will suffice to orient us to the iconographical technique which is everywhere at work in the pages of *Pooh*. Let us proceed to a far weightier matter, one that must be approached in a spirit of combined reverence and determination. *Who is the Savior in this book?* Now, we all realize that no work can be regarded as an immortal classic if it fails to contain a Savior. Shakespeare understood this perfectly well when he invented Cordelia. So did Stephen Crane in *The Red Badge of Courage*,[5] and Faulkner in *Light in August*— both novels that I would, I confess, find altogether repulsive were it not for this winning feature. Must we, in default of a Redeemer, lower *Pooh* in our estimation to the Unitarian or Ethical Culture level? Redoubled study reveals that Milne, with great subtlety, has merely placed the Savior-figure somewhat to one side of the main action, in order to allow the others to fall more spectacularly and

4 Pooh's phrase, "*the wrong sort of bees*," in suggesting that there are two sorts, a right and a wrong, leads us back to the tradition of the medieval encyclopedists who glossed all objects in the universe both *in bonum* and *in malum*, thus providing literary criticism with quite pliant tools of allegorical interpretation. It is a sign of the decadence of our times that this custom has withered away.

5 R. W. Stallman was the first to discover that Jim Conklin in that novel is really Jesus Christ, who brings about "Henry's spiritual change" (Modern Library edition, 1951, Introduction, p. xxxiii), resulting in salvation. I find this admirable insight preferable to Mr. Stallman's remark, one year later, that Henry "has undergone no change, no real spiritual development."—*Stephen Crane: An Omnibus* (New York: Alfred A. Knopf, 1952), p. 221.

thus become ever more tragically aware of their need for Him.[6]

Searching for a literary Savior is, if I may confide in the reader, often a rather trying affair, since this personage must be an epitome of meekness and at the same time act as a strong moral guide for the other characters. In *Pooh* we have no dearth of meek characters, but a frustrating want of moral pronouncements. Yet there is one Character, blessedly, Who outdoes all the others in humility while managing, at one dramatic moment, to reveal His true identity in a divine Uttering: "A little Consideration," He says, "a little Thought for Others, makes all the difference." What an electrifying effect this produces on the reader! At one stroke we have been transported back across all the materialistic heresies of the modern world, back safely across the wicked Counter-Reformation into the purity of Cranmer, Henry the Eighth, the early Church, and the Sermon on the Mount. Here we have none of the hypocrisy of the crafty Loyola, none of the foaming frenzy of the Anabaptists, but a simple assertion of the Golden Rule. The Speaker is of course Eeyore, the Lowly One, the Despised, Acquainted with Grief. His dictum of pure *caritas* is the moral standard by which every action of the lesser characters in *Winnie-the-Pooh* must be severely judged.

Once Eeyore's role has been understood, the reader will naturally be able to perceive innumerable familiar stages in His career. The chapter, "Eeyore Has a Birth-

6 Those doubters who have alleged to find a degree of incompatibility between tragedy and the Christian drama of salvation must be wrong, for tragedy, as the highest form of literature, necessarily contains the highest truth. The typical Christian-tragic hero is buffeted about by Fortune (really Providence in disguise), undergoes from two to five Tragic Insights, expires, and is wafted up to his reward. See Chaucer's *Troilus and Criseyde,* for example.

day," is a charming parallel to the coming of the Magi, with Piglet and Pooh's balloon and pot forming a primitive but nonetheless heartfelt equivalent to frankincense and myrrh. The third gift of gold is supplied by Christopher Robin's generous offer of a box of paints. Eeyore's sermon against washing, "this modern Behind-the-ears nonsense," is His plea that we become as little children, avoiding, by the way, a confusion of materialistic porcelain-and-chrome "progress" with genuine spiritual improvement. "Take no thought for the morrow" would be an approximate rendering of His remark. Again, His placing of His tail in the stream when Roo appears to be drowning is His offer of salvation to all; Milne luckily realized the universal implications of the scene and resisted the opportunity to narrow them down by having only Roo, or indeed anyone, accept the offer. The giving of His own breakfast of thistles to Tigger reminds us of the Loaves and Fishes, but at the same time, to judge from Tigger's reaction, serves as a reminder that the path to Heaven is thorny. His breaking of Tigger's near-fatal *fall from a tree* (italics mine) is, in contrast, a very *exemplum* of the Atonement, while His later contemplation of three sticks forming the letter "A" is an icon at once of the Trinity, the three Cardinal Virtues, and His Own role as the second Adam. His Baptism takes place in the Poohsticks chapter; His Last Supper is the farewell banquet in which He makes the central speech; His exchanging of an earthly home for a Heavenly one occurs in the "Pooh Builds a House" episode; while His Own opening of the gates of the New Jerusalem for all the Saved is bodied forth in "Eeyore Finds the Wolery." Even His Name, as is invariably true in allegorical literature, contains a secret clue to His prototype. A phonetic

transliteration into Italian (the language of sweet Boc-
caccio) yields us IO RE, "I [Am the] King." That the
King should be identified with the lowly Ass is a paradox
which every reader of Scripture will recognize as quin-
tessentially Christian.

Less taxing than the exegetical work I have done above
is the identification of God Himself, namely Christopher
Robin. This is patently evident from His very first inter-
vention in the plot, when, at the end of a week's waiting
(for Pooh to become slender enough to leave Rabbit's
door), He thunders out the single word: *"Now!"* (Italics
God's.) The tone, the delay of a week, and the very
diction leave no doubt that here we have an analogue of
the Creation of Man.[7] In the ensuing chapter, when
Piglet and Pooh have lost themselves in a moral maze of
endless circular error, it is Christopher Robin Who en-
lightens them from Above. As Piglet states with relief at
once, "You'll be quite safe with *him*." Throughout the
book He manifests Himself in the form of Divine Providence, a kind of omnipresent Force at work for the rescue
of the weak and the instruction of the ignorant. Even at
moments of maximum danger, as when Kanga discovers
that her helpless infant is missing, a Peace That Passeth
Understanding calms all fears and erases all forebodings.[8]
As for His Name, this has given me some difficulty, but

---

7 The Vulgate text offers an even clearer sense of this meaning:
"Itaque per hebdomadem Christophorus Robinus librum talem apud
extremitatem septentrionalem Pui praelegit, et Lepus lintea in ex-
tremitate meridiana suspendit . . . et inter eas Pu se ipsum magis
magisque graciliscere sensit. Extremo hebdomadis Christophorus
Robinus dixit: 'NUNC!'" A. A. Milnei, *Winnie Ille Pu* (Novi
Eboraci: Sumptibus Duttonis, MCMLX), p. 22.

8 "Just for a moment, she thought she was frightened, and then
she knew she wasn't; for she felt quite sure that Christopher Robin
would never let any harm happen to Roo."

I recognize within it the following anagram: I HOPE CHRIST BORN. R. I take this to be a decree in the hortatory imperative, dispatched to the Heavenly Host, urging the speedy fulfillment of the Incarnation and signed "R" for REX.[9]

At this point, I believe, everything *essential* has been said about *Winnie-the-Pooh*, and I prefer to draw my explication toward its close. One could, of course, go ever deeper into the book's allegorical subplots, remarking, for instance, the Noah-parallels in the "Surrounded by Water" chapter, studying the Expotition to the North Pole as a Holy Crusade, or laying bare the universal implications of Christopher Robin's nailing the Sacrificial Tail upon the Submissive Eeyore. For myself, I admit, I prefer to leave such matters to more industrious scholars and to contemplate the book in its own terms, as a forthright plea to join the Church of England. Doubtless there will be readers who will continue to laugh indecorously at some of the incidents in *Winnie-the-Pooh*—callous scorners who insist upon taking the chaff and leaving the wheat. My own feelings about this book, if I must say so, are rather more solemn and reverential. I cannot find words to express them, and so will end merely by quoting one of my colleagues who, when faced with the problem of defining and epitomizing the work of another devout writer, Hawthorne, used these words:

The Light is a process of seeing and disclosing; the Word is a process of uttering and investing; the Act is the intuitive union of both. Truth comes as a reward for intellectual dis-

9 That both Eeyore and Christopher Robin thus share the title of "King" will hardly surprise those who have taken the trouble to read the Nicene Creed. "I've got two names," is the very first statement that God makes to Piglet in *Winnie-the-Pooh*.

cipline and human sympathy, but the ultimate incarnation that unites light and letter, spirit and flesh can only *be*.[10]

10 Roy R. Male, *Hawthorne's Tragic Vision* (Austin, Texas: University of Texas Press, 1957), pp. 102f.

QUESTIONS AND STUDY PROJECTS

1. Culpepper seems particularly effective in asserting that *Winnie-the-Pooh* is both *dulcis et utile*, "sweet and useful." Make a list of the ways in which you have used it. Which parts are particularly sweet?

2. Do you feel that Culpepper cites a sufficient number of parallels to demonstrate his allegation about the secret identity of Eeyore? Add to his list of Biblical echoes to make it more convincing, or, if you feel skeptical of his case, make a separate list of parallels proving that Eeyore is really someone else.

MURPHY A. SWEAT

wins every poll hands down when the Yale undergraduates are asked to name their favorite teacher. Many a departing Senior has been heard to say that his course, "Great Modern Writers of My Acquaintance," though "a gut" (rather easy, that is), was "positively the greatest." With his casual dress and warmly appealing platform manner Professor Sweat combines a broad range of learning from virtually every field. In the scholarly world he is well known as Regional Coordinator of University American Studies Programs, Vice-Chairman of the Liberal Arts Deans Committee, Adviser to the Rhodes Scholarship Committee, and President of the Friends of the Yale Crew. Among his many publications we may single out his large Freshman anthology, All Previous Thought, *and his casebooks,* Approaches to Robert W. Service, The Death of Knute Rockne, *and* The Enigma of James Gould Cozzens.

Though the following lecture was later polished and revised for inclusion in Professor Sweat's new edition of Very Great Modern Essays, *your editor has received permission to publish the classroom notes as they were originally delivered, in order to offer outsiders some idea of what it means to be able to go to Yale.*

Winnie and the Cultural Stream

MURPHY A. SWEAT

TODAY I want to tell you guys about a terrific book that you all ought to read for the final exam, if you haven't already. It's very, very big in the English tradition, and has lots of really key things in it. It's called *Winnie-the-Pooh*, and it was written by Al Milne, an English "chap" who took quite a liking to me when I went to see him after the War. He was a real character, but I don't want to go into that—no, no, fellas, really—I've got to give you the scoop on his lit. Let's stick right on the beam today, not like Wednesday when you got me off on those Italian babes I met in the Occupation. We've got to put this bird against the context of his age, you know what I mean?—we've got to get with his world-picture so we can shoot some balanced historical perspective into this *Winnie-the-Pooh*.

Let's see—I guess first off I should tell you that Al's book was for kids, I mean originally, before us longhairs got on to it. Now, of course, everybody's reading it, along with Kafka, Proust, Dostoevski, and the other really big people. Hell, I must have gone through my old copy of *Winnie* a dozen times, psyching out all the cultural cross-references. My kids just read the comics, though; I guess with all the cocktail conversation about Al that they overhear, they figure *Pooh* will be too tough for them. And maybe they're right, too. The fact is, this book can really fool you. You go along, just reading the pages and looking at the pictures, and all of a sudden you say to yourself, Wait a minute! Here's something really *essential*, right on the button for Western Man and the Judeo-Christian tradition. The more you look, the more you find—it's terrible, the amount of thought you've got to put into this thing! So today I'm just going to help you along a little by filling you in on the different levels of meaning in *Winnie* and showing you how it relates to the sociological and politico-economic poop I've been giving you in the other lectures.

One thing you really ought to know for the final is that Al's book came out in 1926. I mean, once you've let that sink in, you see that you've got to look at this thing as part of the Roaring Twenties, the Jazz Age, the Postwar Disillusion, Flappers and Philosophers, Malcolm Cowley, and so on. Otherwise a lot of good dope is going to slip right by you. Like, take this donkey Eeyore. He's really sad, know what I mean? He's worse off than one of you guys when your date from Vassar sends you a flushogram for the Princeton weekend. Well, if you just remember that this was 1926, you see how it all adds up with Hemingway, Faulkner, Dave Lawrence, and the other big ones.

This Eeyore is a dead ringer for Jake Barnes—the one I told you about, with the very serious problem. Or like Popeye in *Sanctuary;* he's just out in left field when it comes down to really basic points. Well, you see, he isn't just any old donkey, but a spokesman for a whole generation—the guys that got a little gassed in the War, the ones who lost their jobs to civilians, the little squirts that got pushed around by the operators, the fellas that came home and found their girls shacked up with somebody else. "History's a nightmare I've been trying to wake up from." That was Joyce, right around the time of *Winnie,* more or less, and it sums up the whole idea I'm trying to get across. That's J-o-y-c-e, James. His Baby Tookums has nothing on Pooh when it comes to really key significance —that's straight from the shoulder!

Now, a few days ago I told you all about the Industrial Revolution and the rise of the middle class. In case you were cutting, the main concept was that this middle class kept rising and rising, see, and this explains all the big developments in European history since around 1600 or so. Then there's this technical changeover, like cotton mills, sports cars, and like that, and the middle class moves right up to the top of the pile. Well, I'd say that *Winnie-the-Pooh* comes right about at the turning point between this rise and the *decline* of the middle class, in favor of other world-historical movements that I'll tell you about next week. The picture we get is of Al sitting down to write this thing just when the bourgeoisie has had its innings. It's just like Proust and those tired-out frogs fifty years ago. So *Winnie,* if you look at it with this special historical poop in mind, turns out to be an ironical commentary on the vacuity (v-a-c-u-i-t-y) of the middle class pretending to have this power that it just doesn't have any more. If you read the book you'll see what I'm driving at. There's this Rabbit, he's the original Bugs Bunny, a real old-time operator—bosses everybody around, signs orders, puts on a big act, like one of you guys heeling the *Yalie Daily*. And where does it get him? It looks simple, see, but no matter how hard he tries he can't snow these other characters too well. I mean, the point is, these old managers and bosses, the inner-directed ones, are washed up in the modern world where everybody's got to hang together, like old Ben Franklin said.

Now, one big thing you always have to watch out for in literature is the tragic vision. An author without a tragic vision is like a WYBC announcer without a mike. Look at Sophocles; look at Shakespeare; look at Arthur Miller; they've *all* got one. Let's not overlook the Great Chain of Being, either. I told you about that one, with God at the top and all these little vegetables and rocks down at the bottom. Everybody got that straight? Well, it's all right there in *Winnie*, too. It's a kind of hierarchy of heroism, that's the way I'd phrase it personally. You've got Pooh and Christopher Robin at the top—that's right, "Christopher Robin," I admit he sounds like a fairy but it's too early to tell—and then all the others in the middle, going down to Small and Alexander Beetle. You don't stand a chance of grabbing the concepts in this book if you don't line it up with this Chain of Being. As for the tragic vision, you get pretty well buried in it at the end, when Cwistopha Wobin has to say bye-bye to his widdle teddy bear. It breaks you up the first time, but after that you can sit back and zoom in on all the parallels with *Oedipus at Colonus*.

Of course, you don't want to forget that *Winnie* is a modern, up-to-date book as well as a "classic." I'm sure you remember all the characteristics of the modern novel, since you worked them up for the first hour test. I know you won't get it confused with the Victorian novel, which is inter-class mobility, the wisdom of the heart, the Darwinian Revolution, Herbert Spencer, the twilight of religion, tears, idle tears, and the responsibility of Empire. What I'm talking about is the vanishing hero, alienation, *Angst*, symbolism, the interior monologue and the stream of consciousness. Look, here's a quotation, see if you can identify it:

After all, . . . Christopher Robin depends on Me. He's fond of Pooh and Piglet and Eeyore, and so am I, but they haven't any Brain. Not to notice. And he respects Owl, because you can't help respecting anybody who can spell TUESDAY, even if he doesn't spell it right; but spelling isn't everything. There are days when spelling Tuesday simply doesn't count. And Kanga is too busy looking after Roo, and Roo is too young and Tigger is too bouncy to be any help, so there's really nobody but Me, when you come to look at it. I'll go and see if there's anything he wants doing, and then I'll do it for him. It's just the day for doing things.

Is that Dotsy Richardson? Ginny Woolf? Is it Poldy Bloom thinking about Gertie McDowell? No, it's Rabbit! Absolutely right up to date with all the most respected devices of style! As for *Angst*, I would put Winnie right up near the top, along with Kierkegaard, Sartre, and the other big minds of the twentieth century. You can read Ionesco and Beckett backwards and forwards, but you won't get as much sense of the Absurd as one page of *Winnie* gives you, with all those questions about Backsons and Woozles and nobody knows what's really up. Let's not forget the sexual element either; there's no danger of you guys forgetting that, is there? This Tigger, well, there's nothing in Grace Metalious that can lay a glove on him for potency. He's like one of those bulls or horses that Lawrence used to go so ape over. Of course, he

doesn't see much action, you've got to remember the kiddies' angle in this book, but if you read between the lines you'll see what the score is quick enough. (Now I *know* you fellas will read it!)

Now, another way to size up *Winnie*—I'm just sort of closing in on it from all sides so you won't miss any tricks—is the "genre" bit. That sounds like Johnner but you spell it g-e-n-r-e, and it means what kind of lit you want to line it up along with. It looks easy, but here as usual you've got to keep on your toes. Like, *Moby-Dick* is the novel genre, but it's also the epic genre too, since it has: (1) lofty language, (2) grand heroism, (3) geographical sweep, (4) supernatural reference, and (5) noble purpose. This kind of problem has been stumping us in the novel ever since Fielding pulled that dirty one of saying his book was a "comic epic in prose"; that put us critics on the ropes and we're still reeling. Well, *Winnie* is no exception. First, it's a novel all right, since it's got prose, characters and action, lengthiness (if you put both books together), and psychological development. It definitely squeezes under the wire as a novel. But then it's a gasser too, so you have to say it's a comedy. Then, since nothing very exciting really happens, and everyone is jumping around this happy little forest all the time, we've got to work in the pastoral. Pastoral is a very important genre that taxed the creative powers of some of the really hot writers in olden times, like Virgil and Milton. Well, Al may have been a sucker to try his hand at it, but that's his problem; it's our job as critics just to say that *Winnie is* a pastoral. "NCP" is what you ought to remember for the final, Novel-Comedy-Pastoral, and this should put you in the clear.

Before you snap up your old spring binders and head for lunch, there's one or two more key items you ought to swallow. You can't honestly say you've doped out *Winnie* until you've soaked up a little of the philosophic development of the plot. I know that you fellas don't have enough time to really toss yourselves into knotty questions like this—especially you guys that are bushed every night after working out with the Squad—so I'll just fire the general picture at you myself. You see, the thing that separates a really big, important novel from a regular throwaway is the philosophic development of the plot. Take *The Magic Mountain*, by Tom Mann. It's about this bunch of birds who sit around an old health resort wondering if they're going to croak. Some do, some don't, and then the book is over. If it weren't for the philosophic development of the plot this would be the most boring thing since Orientation Week. But if you size up this philosophic development you see it's really all about Western Man, humanism, science, Freud, *Liebestod*, and stuff like that, and you've *got* to admit it's good, whether you like it or not. I saw Tom last week and he told me he put a hell of a lot of work into making it all hang together. Now, if we pass the ball to Al we see that he can run with it too. If you think *Winnie*'s lightweight stuff, you've got another think coming. The fact is, this book develops some of the really central antitheses of our time. Like, Capitalism versus Communism: look at the way all the good, free characters are played off against that dumb herd of Rabbit's friends and relations who're always together and never talk back. Or like, Prose versus Poetry: Al keeps you guessing which one he's going to spring on you. Or like, Men versus Women: look at all that business about trying to ease Kanga out of the Forest. This is just the beginning, of course. If I had more time I'd show you just how all this works out, step by step. Thesis, Synthesis, and Antithesis is usually the way I put it myself, this developmental concept. Maybe we can get in a few licks at it on Monday.

Let's wind this up with a few words from the late Bill Faulkner. I was with him when he died, and he said to me, "Murph, when the last ding-dong of doom has ding-dung, folks will still be a-readin' *Winnie-the-Pooh*. I've writ a passel a' novels but this 'un beats 'em all. You be shore 'n tell the fellers at Yale all 'bout it." Well, I guess I won't try to improve on a tribute like that. You've got the poop on *Pooh* now, and it's up to you to come across and fill up your bluebooks with it on the final. Don't get too loaded over the weekend now, and let's see everybody out there at the Bowl on Saturday to support the Squad!

QUESTIONS AND STUDY PROJECTS

1. Some members of your class may have noticed that Professor Sweat's lecturing style has a lively, "zippy" pace not common in the other selections. Try to ascertain what stylistic devices Sweat used in order to achieve this engaging tone, and write an essay on "*Winnie*" in the same "rip-roaring," "down-to-earth" manner.

2. Write a comparison of the critical method of Sweat and Window *or* Sweat and Honeycomb *or* Sweat and Masterson *or* Masterson-and-Sweat versus Honeycomb-and-Window. The more conscientious students will doubtless find it irresistible to try *all* these combinations.

WOODBINE MEADOWLARK

describes himself frankly as "a perpetual graduate student." Though his face and name have become legendary in Harvard Yard over the years, and though he is praised by all his teachers, he has never bothered to present himself for his doctor's orals. "I love literature too deeply to put up with the botanizing that is done upon it in graduate work," he explains. "I attend some classes here and there, but I insist upon remaining a free spirit, unfettered by academic routine. Literature is the very breath of my life; and, as I happen to have an independent income, I can afford to live exactly as the caprices of my whimsy dictate." The following essay, which once circulated in manuscript among Mr. Meadowlark's most intimate friends, is said to have found its way to an editor's desk by sheerest accident, without the author's knowledge. Since its first appearance, however, it has been reprinted several times.

A la recherche du Pooh perdu

BY

WOODBINE MEADOWLARK

THERE are few stories, whether written for adults or for children, more poignantly affecting than *Winnie-the-Pooh*. I remember how, at the age of seven, my Aunt Amelia slipped a copy of the book into my little hands and, with a smile that perhaps betrayed a suppressed tear for the lost beauties of childhood, said, "Woodbine, you will read many a book before your time is over, for you are an aesthetic child; but you will never read anything one-eighth so moving as *Winnie-the-Pooh*." I shall never forget my Aunt Amelia, not only because it was she who established the independent income upon which I am now subsisting comfortably, but because she brought into my little life this precious volume. Since that day, just as she predicted, I have cherished many books—*Marius the Epicurean, A Child in the House,* and *Other Voices, Other Rooms,* to name a few. *Pooh,* however, remains my favorite, and in these following pages, written only for certain eyes to delectate—God forbid they should ever submit to the cruel embrace of the printing press—I pay my tribute to the cause of so many tender hours of bittersweet reading.

What, let me first ask myself, is exactly the tone, the quality of expression, that prevails in *Winnie-the-Pooh,* lending the entire volume that subtle sadness which simultaneously enervates and thrills? The answer is *Weltschmerz*—a profound *Schmerz* whose implications are reverberatingly universal. And whence comes this *Weltschmerz?* From the atmosphere of alienation, of uncertainty and mystery, of tragic estrangement from reality, that Milne has everywhere suffused into his narrative. Whether or not this has been perceived by more "professional" critics I would not know; I certainly could never bear to scan the body of venal commentary that is said to have grown up around the book in recent times. I know only what my insights tell me—insights sharpened, I must say, through myriad rereadings, insights which I hope will be deemed clear even though they were conceived when my eyes were blurred with emotion.

The world of *Pooh* is, of course, that of childhood writ large. Childhood, you say? Gaiety, Song-and-Dance, the Social Round of birthday parties and treasure hunts? No, no, my friends; the essence of childhood is melancholy. What is a child, if not a being cut off tragically from real knowledge, yearning to know the secrets of the adult world but being appeased, at best, with half-truths and condescension? The child must content himself with his own few poignant relationships to his fellow children, and try to live with his terrifyingly distorted

impressions of his parents, nurses, gardeners, and foot-
men. At the same time, he is doubly alienated by the
failure of his elders to understand *him*. What would they
—preoccupied as they are with their country club, their
stables, their stock dividends—what would they, I say,
know about that dawning imagination which conceives
of the entire universe as its little bathtub to splash in—
which colors every slightest object with the pink cherubic
glow of childish affection?

This, then, is to be the atmosphere of *Winnie-the-Pooh*,
announced, whimsically enough, at the outset when
Christopher Robin (*dear* little fellow!) has bumped his
teddy bear down the stairs and looked up with limpid
misunderstanding at his father. When the elder Milne
hears that the bear's name is Winnie, he asks,

"But I thought he was a boy?"

"So did I," said Christopher Robin.

"Then you can't call him Winnie?"

"I don't."

"But you said—"

"He's Winnie-ther-Pooh. Don't you know what 'ther'
means?"

"Ah, yes, now I do," I said quickly; and I hope you do too,
because it is all the explanation you are going to get.

Here the reader, as well as Christopher Robin and his
father, is enjoined not to try to cross the impassable
border between the two pathetically separated worlds.
Milne, in pretending to understand his son, is saying to
us in effect, Reader! If you wish to be granted any slightest glimpse into the juvenile fancy, please refrain from
casting upon it the hard, cold light of logical reason. Do
not demand explanations, but offer up your soul, for a
few golden hours, to the charm and magic of lost hori-

zons—horizons once known to you, too, but long since disappeared among the daily affairs and impure desires of adulthood. *Winnie-the-Pooh*, then, is to be a story told, as much as possible, from the child's point of view, and much of its wry appeal stems from the respectful restraint we feel ourselves exercising in accepting the naïve assumptions of Christopher Robin. Much of the *Weltschmerz*, likewise, derives from this very convention, for in looking at the world through Christopher's eyes we see again, what we once felt all too vividly, the otherness of grownups and the unavailability of true knowledge.

In this light *Winnie-the-Pooh*, while it is quite devoid of any literary affectation (a thing I cannot abide), is nevertheless redolent of the most "modern" atmosphere; for the wall that is set up between parent and child is an ideal figure for the wall of non-communication we now know to exist between man and man—to say nothing of the *total* hopelessness of contact between man and woman. (May I add, parenthetically, that part of the loveliness of childhood, namely the charming ambivalence between male and female, is embodied in the passage I have quoted above?) No modern symbolist, imagist, or surrealist could have found better scenes to body forth his anguish than some of those in *Winnie-the-Pooh*. Consider the spurious hunt for the Heffalump and the later puzzle over the Spotted or Herbaceous Backson—mythical beasts, both of them, that have been conjured up by the nameless fears and suspicions of infancy, and which can be dispelled (and then only partially) solely by the reassurance of our elders. The most perfect emblem of ignorance is contained in the "Woozle" scene, which gives us Pooh and Piglet (ethereal, purehearted Piglet, the real hero of the book) wandering helplessly in circles, following their own darling little tracks and misconceiving their goal ever more thoroughly as they proceed. Is this not the very essence of modern man. aching with existential *nausée* and losing himself more deeply in despair as his longing for certainty waxes?

It is, then, in a world of this tonal quality that the real, inner drama of *Winnie-the-Pooh* unfolds. And just what is this drama? What is the subtle play of meaning that knits the *Pooh* volumes together with consummate artistry and leaves us at the end with a sense of conclusion, a sense that something has, after all, been decided? I reply that these books deal, fundamentally, with a debate over true wisdom and an attempt to arrest the clock at the wisdom of childhood. The wisdom of childhood is, of course, the mystic capacity to live only in the present moment, to burn with a hard, gemlike flame, to drain to the dregs the cup of life and never ask where the next drop may come from. This rejection of future time as well as past time, this reveling in the actual, is the kingdom of heaven promised, I am afraid delusively, by religion but realizable in every child at any possible moment of the day. "A six years' Darling of a pygmy size!"

sang Wordsworth, making the very point I am trying to
express:

> *Mighty Prophet! Seer blest!*
> *On whom those truths do rest,*
> *Which we are toiling all our lives to find,*
> *In darkness lost, the darkness of the grave . . .*

A. A. Milne, of course, no less than Wordsworth, finds
himself unable to recapture this lost wisdom, and, what
is more, he is keenly aware that Christopher Robin himself must soon abandon it for a more practical, mundane
outlook. The drama of the book is just the wistful process
of doubting, reaffirming, and finally losing altogether the
possibility of a permanent childhood, an eternal spree in
the sole company of one's teddy bears. There is nothing
in literature to match this pathetic development, unless
it be Marcel's vain effort to call Albertine back to life.
In the field of painting it is comparable only to the sub-
limest triumphs of Rossetti and Burne-Jones.

The wisdom of childhood is, of course, most unequivocally defended, not in the *Pooh* books, which put it to
the test, but in the earlier *When We Were Very Young.*
You should look at a poem called "Spring Morning" for
a pure expression of it. The poem extols the absolute lack
of planning in a child's day, the freedom of heart that
enables him to wander in any direction with equal joy. It
concludes:

> *Where am I going? I don't quite know.*
> *What does it matter where people go?*
> *Down to the wood where the blue-bells grow—*
> *Anywhere, anywhere. I don't know.*

This, you see, is the innocence of intention that Christo-

pher Robin, like every other child who must be torn
away from his loving mum and handed over to the stern
governess and thence to school, is destined to lose. In
Winnie-the-Pooh it is best represented in the person of
Pooh himself, who neither can, nor wishes to, think ahead
more than a few minutes, and who can be distracted in
most endearing fashion from anything he happens to
have begun. In contrast to the relatively "adult" and
repellent Rabbit, who "never let things come to him,"
Pooh is essentially passive, a recipient, like Shelley, of
inspiration from the very winds. In the struggle of values
lying just beneath the surface of the book's plot, Pooh
symbolizes this ideal for Christopher Robin, while Rabbit
and Owl stand for the opposite: self-important "maturity," nervous busyness. It is obvious that Milne prefers
Pooh's mode of living, and the point is made again and
again. For example:

> "Rabbit's clever," said Pooh thoughtfully.
> "Yes," said Piglet, "Rabbit's clever."
> "And he has Brain."
> "Yes," said Piglet, "Rabbit has Brain."
> There was a long silence.
> "I suppose," said Pooh, "that that's why he never under-
> stands anything."

Thus we see established, among the very personages in
Christopher Robin's toy world, a dramatic play of phi-
losophies, the force of which seems to be to confirm
Christopher Robin in his choice of freedom and innocence. For Christopher himself takes Pooh's side against
Owl and Rabbit, demonstrating by his actions in the
story that Owl's learning and Rabbit's meddlesomeness
need not prevail. The very sounds of the Forest, this

Forest of childhood purity, are marshaled to preserve the mystic moment: they all say to the drowsy Pooh, "Don't listen to Rabbit, listen to me." Pooh listens, and so, too, does Christopher Robin as long as he can. Even a few pages from the heart-rending close of *The House at Pooh Corner* he can still affirm his belief in doing "Nothing," which he defines as "just going along, listening to all the things you can't hear, and not bothering."

Alas! Exquisitely beautiful as this divine indolence is, it cannot withstand the simple, unrelenting assault of time, which sweeps every living thing toward atrophy and death. Pooh, being a toy rather than a person, is exempt from the process; his clock is symbolically stopped forever—a fact ecstatically Keatsian—at five minutes to eleven, the hour for contemplating a snack. Nor are the other animals concerned about senescence. But Christopher Robin is a mortal, and to be mortal means, of very necessity, to grow old and die. The symbol of creeping death in *Winnie-the-Pooh* is schoolwork, with all its implications of programmatic study, looking to the future, choosing a career, and therefore plunging toward a final annihilation. Christopher cannot postpone this sequence; the most he can do is to pretend that his freedom will endure, as when he comes down to the game of Pooh-sticks "feeling all sunny and careless, and just as if twice nineteen didn't matter a bit . . ." Yet the very stream he is approaching is the stream of time, which will swirl Eeyore around and around in helpless circles, but take Christopher's "Poohstick" and send it hurtling straight down to the great all-absorbing sea of destruction.

It is only with the strongest effort of will that I can bring myself to speak of the final chapter of *The House at Pooh Corner*. My first reading of it brought on an

acute attack of asthma, from which I have periodically
suffered ever since; and Mummy used to tell me before
she herself was swept away by cirrhosis of the liver, that
I should take up something healthier than literature,
perhaps croquet or fencing. But it is too late; I regard
this chapter as a part of my own biography, and I have
relived it so many times that once more—however painful—will make little difference in the long run. The last
chapter, then, is Christopher Robin's farewell, not merely
to childhood, but to the wisdom of the mystic present.
Like another wrenching farewell, Shakespeare's in *The
Tempest*, it brings to a height all the magical power of
fancy and then, at a certain moment, blows it into
nothingness. *Tempest*-like, indeed, is the way "these our
actors," who at one instant are gathered in an embarrassed
circle around Christopher Robin, suddenly "are melted
into air, into thin air." No one is left of the group but
Pooh, and he has been spared only to suffer the unkindest
cut of all, a direct farewell from Christopher Robin. Christopher's behavior leaves nothing to be desired for childish
purity of motive: he swears eternal loyalty to Pooh, makes
Pooh his Faithful Knight, and promises to meet him again
in the timeless "Enchanted Place." Yet we know with
exquisitely grievous certainty that these are last gestures,
last desperate efforts to save something from the wrack
of his childish dreams. Even Pooh realizes, with tragic
resignation, that the cloud-capped towers are disappear-
ing:

Then he began to think of all the things Christopher Robin
would want to tell him when he came back from wherever
he was going to, and how muddling it would be for a Bear of
Very Little Brain to try and get them right in his mind. "So,
perhaps," he said sadly to himself, "Christopher Robin won't

tell me any more," and he wondered if being a Faithful Knight meant that you just went on being faithful without being told things.

All, all has been lost; and when we come to the last pitiful sentence of the book, in which Milne asserts that in some sense Pooh and Christopher Robin "will always be playing" in the Enchanted Place, we are not deceived. The sentence takes on its full meaning only as we grasp its purpose of providing a counterweight to the inexorable pull of temporality that is dashing Christopher Robin away from us forever. It is unbearable, unbearable! and I myself, whenever I have reread it and felt myself once

again swept onto Matthew Arnold's darkling plain of aloneness, prefer to turn for consolation to the last lines of *Now We Are Six*:

> *But now I am Six, I'm as clever as clever.*
> *So I think I'll be six now for ever and ever.*

QUESTIONS AND STUDY PROJECTS

1. Meadowlark asserts that Piglet is the real hero of *Winnie-the-Pooh*. How does Piglet compare to *four* of the following heroes: Achilles, Job, Beowulf, Lord Nelson, Natty Bumppo, Captain Ahab, David Copperfield, Frank Merriwell, Sergeant York, and Augie March?

2. Is Meadowlark necessarily correct in asserting that true wisdom and formal education act at cross-purposes? If this is true at your college, perhaps you could suggest reforms in the curriculum to bring it more in line with "those truths" possessed by the "mighty prophet" and "seer blest" in Wordsworth's Ode. Perhaps the physical sciences and engineering, which absorb such a large portion of college budgets these days, should be the first subjects for reappraisal in this light. What do *you* think?

DUNS C. PENWIPER,

an Iowan originally, received his A.B., M.A., and Ph.D. degrees from the University of Chicago, where he has subsequently passed through the ranks of Instructor, Assistant Professor, and Associate Professor. His dissertation, The Wind in the Willows and the Tradition of Medieval Rhetoric, *was published recently by the University of Chicago Press and reviewed favorably in* Modern Philology. *Professor Penwiper is unceasingly grateful for the humanistic perspectives and training in critical technique he received as an undergraduate, and he makes a point of dedicating all his work, including the present article, to "the devoted teachers who showed me that making structural definitions is one of the highest activities of man."*

A Complete Analysis of
Winnie-the-Pooh

BY

DUNS C. PENWIPER

NO ANALYSIS of a literary work, *Winnie-the-Pooh* not excepted, can, in this age of conflicting critical schools, afford not to rest itself upon a thorough consideration of methodological principles. Of the four possible general attitudes, or approaches to the critical approach, that it is possible to take—*viz.*, the dogmatic, the syncretistic, the skeptical, and the instrumentalistic— no sober critic will choose other than the fourth. Given our instrumentalistic pluralism, however, we must not commit ourselves hastily to regarding all possible exegetical tools as of equal value. Criticism, after all, being nothing more nor less than reasoned discourse, must successfully integrate propositions, refutations, and literally discriminable functions with sound hypothetical causal inference, and from this it follows that the operational

devices of each system are open to evaluation on the
grounds of their relative capacity for rhetorical communication in its three useful branches, to wit, full compre-
hension of subject matter, logical presentation of data,
and effective contact with audience. In this light almost
all the methodologies we might otherwise be tempted to
sample appear inadequate and dangerous; whatever good
results they may have produced "have been achieved,"
as R. S. Crane puts it, "to a considerable extent in spite
of the critics' addiction to principles of inquiry and
knowledge the limited range and restricted capacity for
development of which are at the very least not matters
for self-congratulation." [1]

The critical technique which must, when considered
in the light of reason, form the core of our eclectic, in-
strumentalistically pluralistic *principia* recommends itself
to us at once if we merely pose the question, what, in
essence, is the end purpose, the teleology, of poetry or
poesis? It is, of course, to take the building blocks of
language, combined with the glue or mortar of experience, and to join them in whole meaningful structures
which, upon noesis on the part of the trained critic,
prove analyzable or decomposable into their constituent
elements. We thus see that without structural analysis,
such as it was practiced by Aristotle and refined by his
modern disciples, poetry itself would be missing fully
half its definition. That this applies equally to *Winnie-
the-Pooh* would, I believe, be not unsuperfluous to add,
even in a study devoting itself single-mindedly, as the
present one does, to exhaustive criticism of that literary
production.

[1] R. S. Crane (ed.), *Critics and Criticism, Ancient and Modern*
(Chicago: University of Chicago Press, 1952). Introduction, p. 10.

It may not be totally unenlightening in an *investigatio* of this kind if we give one or two of the innumerable reasons for this critical preference. It is partly by comparison with the deficiencies of recent schools that we see the classic beauty of the Aristotelian. For, as R. S. Crane has justly lamented, "it is hard to think of any period in the long history of criticism in which the analytical concepts employed by most practical critics have been fewer in number or more abstract." [2] This, I think, strikes at the heart of the trouble: *a distressing scarcity of terminology*. It is a problem over which we might well lament, were it not for the saving fact that in the Neo-Aristotelian school we can find a veritable cornucopia of terms. I am thinking not only of the *Poetics*, which certainly provides an abundant beginning, but also of the myriad concepts and entities that must be linguistically formulated in order to cope with post-Aristotelian literary genres, to say nothing, of course, of the terms needed to explicate the doubtful points in Aristotle himself. The Aristotelian analytic method is thus "comprehensive," in Professor Crane's words,

by virtue of the devices it affords for discriminating a posteriori an indefinite number of different poetic forms or principles of construction and for dealing differentially with the common elements these involve, in terms not merely of their material content or technical configuration but of the functions they can be made to serve, directly or indirectly, in the constitution of different kinds of poetic wholes; with the result that, when the method is properly used, it permits a far wider range of relevant differentiations in the discussion not only of poems but of poetic devices and materials than any method in which such a functional treatment of elements has no place.[3]

2 *Ibid.*, Introduction, p. 15.   3 *Ibid.*, Introduction, p. 20.

This method, then, which Elder Olson has defined as "one of multiple differentiation and systematic resolution of maximal composites into their least parts,"[4] opens up virtually limitless perspectives of methodological and analytical terms, all admirably suited for exploring the very heart of the *synola,* or artistic wholes, that writers have been kind enough to turn over to us.

Scarcely less important than terminological reasons for relying on Aristotelianism (and we shall forge ahead with *Pooh* in just a moment) are considerations of general range. Nothing is more alarming, in reading the criticism of other schools, than to see how narrow, rigid, and dogmatic an approach is usually taken to the extremely complex task of analysis. Our own method, in marked contrast, may justly lay claim to being virtually universal in scope. "Comprehensive," again, is the word Professor Crane aptly chooses. Nothing whatever is excluded from Aristotelianism, he explains, except

the whole complex of accidental causes of variation in poetry that depend on the talents, characters, educations, and intentions of individual authors, the opinions and tastes of the audiences they address, the state of the language in their time, and all the other external factors which affect their choice of materials and conventions in particular works.[5]

From this the reader will easily perceive that, no matter how many terms we coin or borrow from Aristotle, our field of inquiry is so vast that entire encyclopedias of definitions, categories, entities, rhetorical terms, methodological principles, and metaphysical frameworks could

4 Elder Olson, "An Outline of Poetic Theory," *ibid.,* p. 560.
5 Crane, *ibid.,* Introduction, p. 20.

not begin to exhaust it. It is only natural that we at Chicago should be proud of our critical equipment—proud but not, I trust, smug or self-inflated. Preferring Aristotle to anyone else is merely, as Professor Crane says, "like a modern physicist's preference for Einsteinian over Newtonian concepts"; [6] it is a perfectly objective choice of right over wrong that bears no slightest trace of personal involvement or condescension.

We are now prepared, I believe, to return to *Winnie-the-Pooh* with some philosophical confidence that we know what we are about. It is clear that the object of study here (the artistic whole qua artistic whole) falls essentially into the category of art, or broadly speaking, *poesis*. We may thus set ourselves the all-important task of deciding just which, among the many potential forms of art, inhabits the essential entelechy of *Pooh*. We are obviously in need of some formation of this possible range. Such a formulation is offered us in the succinct words of Richard McKeon:

Poetry may be conceived as vision, contriving, or imitation, experience, imagination, or emotion, symbol, action, or relation. Any one of these may be generalized or specified to determine a sense in which all men, or the best of men, or the best of some peculiarly fortunate kind of men, are poets or poems, since the traits of the poet or the structure or contents of the poem are universally those of mankind or even of the Deity and the universe or since the poem or its expression or the emotion it embodies is universally intelligible or universally moving or corresponds with and reflects aspects of the universe or since its effects are homogeneous with the common experience or aspirations of mankind.[7]

6 *Ibid.*, Introduction, p. 13.
7 Richard McKeon, "The Philosophic Bases of Art and Criticism," *ibid.*, p. 472.

I think everyone will agree that *Winnie-the-Pooh* falls under the fourth of Professor McKeon's rubrics given here. Let us then pass on to other matters.

We must now come to grips with the fact that *Winnie-the-Pooh*, if it is truly an artistic work of the sort described above, must contain the three main properties of art-works, *viz.*, unity, imitation, and beauty. The unity of a work consists fundamentally in the mutual adherence of its parts within a total conspectus of form which, while allowing for variety among separate elements, yet contains those elements and, furthermore, contains no other elements that might make a disunified effect. *Winnie-the-Pooh* fully meets this requirement. With regard to imitation, we must rely on Elder Olson's admirable observation:

The term "imitation" is used coextensively with "artificial"; it differentiates art from nature. Natural things have an internal principle of motion and rest, whereas artificial things—a chair or a table—have, qua products of arts, no such principle; they change through propensities not of their form but of their matter.[8]

The problem here is thus seen to be that of verifying the tentative hypothesis that *Winnie-the-Pooh* has no internal principle of motion or rest. I have pondered this very carefully and considered the question from many sides, and it is my judgment that the book is, indeed, artificial, and hence a product of imitation.

As for beauty, this takes us far afield in the subtleties of Aristotelianism. We may begin with Professor Olson's definition:

By "beauty" I mean the excellence of perceptible form in a composite continuum which is a whole; and by "excellence of

8 Elder Olson, "An Outline of Poetic Theory," *ibid.*, p. 553.

perceptible form" I mean the possession of perceptible magnitude in accordance with a mean determined by the whole as a whole of such-and-such quality, composed of such-and-such parts. Assuming that parts of the number and quality required for the whole have been provided and ordered hierarchically to the principal part, the whole will be beautiful if that prime part is beautiful; and that part, as a continuity, must have magnitude and be composed of parts (e.g., plot, the prime part of tragedy, has magnitude and has parts); since it has magnitude, it admits of the more and the less, and hence of excess and deficiency, and consequently of a definite and proper mean between them, which constitutes its beauty.[9]

The reader will have noted the emphasis here upon the key term, "magnitude," which is altogether indispensable to literary criticism. As Professor Olson explains a bit farther on, a poem "must have a certain definite magnitude as determined by the specific whole and its parts; and the proper magnitude will be the fullest extension possible, not exceeding the limits mentioned above, and accomplished by phases connected necessarily or probably." [10] The importance of this criterion strikes us vividly in Norman Maclean's dictum that "For a piece of writing to have its proper size is an excellent thing." [11] We must, then, if we are to determine whether *Winnie-the-Pooh* meets the requirement of beauty, first decide whether it is of the proper magnitude—not too little and not too much, but just enough.

Unfortunately, this answer must wait upon an intervening concern. There is no infallible method of estimating a poem's magnitude other than to feel the magnitude's

9 *Ibid.*, p. 556.
10 *Ibid.*, p. 565.
11 Norman Maclean, "Episode, Scene, Speech, and Word: The Madness of Lear," *ibid.*, p. 596.

appropriateness or inappropriateness in an actual reading. Now, this *reading* of the work introduces new complications that might not otherwise have entered into our critical method. As Professor Olson says, "Inference and perception serve to institute opinions and mental images concerning the object, and opinions and mental images produce emotion." [12] This psychological theory, which, incidentally, concurs entirely with the latest formulations of Hobbes and Locke, brings us onto the ground of the emotions, where we at Chicago happen to be particularly strong. We divide all emotions into mental pains, pleasures, and impulses instigated by opinion. From these categories we derive the following schemes of imitation in poetry: the serious and the comic. From these (and I continue to follow Professor Olson here) further subdivisions are precipitated: the tragic and the punitive, and the lout-comic and the rogue-comic. Between these extremes we have also succeeded in isolating two other types, the sympathetic and the antipathetic, and various further categories as well; but for the moment it may be well to pause at this point and reintroduce *Winnie-the-Pooh*. Close examination of the text informs us that this book is of the lout-comic subdivision of the comic species, and, being of essentially pleasant subject matter, produces pleasure directly as opposed to the cathartic or purgative method. In short, *Winnie-the-Pooh* is funny. With this conclusion we may go back to confront the problem of magnitude, and in doing so we discover, to our great relief, that *Winnie-the-Pooh* is of exactly the proper magnitude for a funny book. Hence it logically follows that *Winnie-the-Pooh* is beautiful.

Though we have now come far in our study, there is

12 Olson, *ibid.*, p. 554.

yet further cause for making structural discriminations. If everything about an art-work may be classified under one of the headings, object, means, manner, and effect, we see that we have only fully satisfied the topics of object and effect; that is, *Winnie-the-Pooh* is a beautiful, unified, imitative book (object) and a funny book (effect). We have still to discuss the other two terms that are left when object and effect have been subtracted; to wit, means and manner. To guide us at this crucial point we may call again on Professor McKeon:

The subject matter of discussion of art is determined by three considerations which bear on things and which depend on principles: first, the determination of the kind of things appropriate to the discussion is stated in general philosophic principles; second, the determination of the mode of classifying such things depends on the methodological definition of principles; third, the determination of the characteristics relevant to the evaluation of such things is stated in the principles of criticism.[13]

Since we already know, first, what kind of things we wish to discuss, secondly, what our general philosophic principles are, and thirdly, what our methodological definition of principles is, we would appear to be justified in simply tossing caution to the winds and seizing boldly upon the object that will most directly help us to determine the means and manner of *Winnie-the-Pooh*—*id est*, the plot.

Of Aristotle's six terms for describing tragedy, *viz.*, plot, character, thought, diction, melody, and spectacle, by far the most important is plot. Upon the successful use of this term, as Professor McKeon reminds us, "the

13 McKeon, *ibid.*, p. 478.

possibility of a poetic science depends." [14] Now, the great contribution that Aristotle made to our understanding of the concept of plot was his discovery that a plot should have, first, a beginning; secondly, a middle; and last but not least, an end. This is the *sine qua non* of an excellent plot. As Professor Crane says of a great English novel, "It is in nothing short of this total system of actions, moving by probable or necessary connections from beginning, through middle, to end, that the unity of the plot of *Tom Jones* is to be found." [15] It is thus imperative that we discover these elements in *Winnie-the-Pooh*. Picking up the volume and scanning the opening pages, we verify the existence of a beginning; with increasing delight at the author's art we find ourselves, roughly halfway through, at the middle; and finally, marveling at the power, or *dynamis*, of the artist to inform the very void and chaos of his material with sublime order, we perceive on the last page that we have reached the end.

Now, all plots may be divided into the two classes of simple and complex. Since *Winnie-the-Pooh* was written at the third of the three stages through which the history of art passes—I refer to the instinctive, the ethical or practical, and the artistic [16]—we should expect its plot to be complex, and so it is. We can, following Aristotle, identify a complex plot by recognizing its differentiable parts, to wit, peripety and discovery; and we find ample portions of both in *Winnie-the-Pooh*. We distinguish peripety from discovery according to the efficient cause of the change of fortunes involved, and here again we discover that *Winnie-the-Pooh*, abounding as it does in

14 *Ibid.*, p. 534.

15 Crane, "The Concept of Plot and the Plot of *Tom Jones*," *ibid.*, p. 631.

16 See Olson, *ibid.*, p. 558.

efficient causes of both varieties, confirms our impression that it is a work of the highest art. We can now go on to classify the plot more exactly. Of the four kinds of action that are possible—I mean, a single character in a closed situation, two or more characters in a closed situation, a collection of such scenes (i.e., an episode), and a system of such episodes—we discover that *Pooh* belongs to the fourth. In other words, it is a true plot and must be ranked along with the *Iliad* and *Hamlet* in this respect.

Finally, we may conclude this analysis—begging the reader's indulgence for the length at which we have dwelt upon some of the more serious problems of form and meaning in *Pooh*—by anatomizing a typical plot situation in the book. If we let A stand for one of the characters, B for a second, and C (following out the established pattern of consecutive form) for a third, we see that there are various situations in *Winnie-the-Pooh* employing some of the most complicated devices of plot known to criticism. A's relationship to B is often such that C, who had hoped to establish a certain contact with B, finds himself constrained instead to deal with A. Or again, C may initiate an action against A; A replies by appealing to B; B thinks over the matter to himself, decides not to act, and departs; C and A are thus left on the scene to resolve their differences, either by C's reconciling himself to A, A's reconciling himself to C, or A's (or C's) undertaking a decisive finishing action *against* the other. Still more intricate are the plot situations in which A, B, and C have nothing whatever to say to each other, but are obliged to remain together on barely amicable terms until the end of the episode. This we call the "Jamesian" situation, which draws its complexity from the subtleties of appeal, criticism, muted disrespect, and barbed repartee among the characters involved. And to finish our survey, we must not omit the type of situation in which A, B, and C, preoccupied by a common problem, set off together and are joined by D, E, and F (standing for further characters in the plot); G, H, and I then arrive, accompanied by J, K, and L. Soon, in the company of M, N, and O, the other characters set off to discover either a particular object or place, or the further characters P, Q, and R; and when this has been successfully done the entire group, from A through R, sits down to a hearty lunch.

Here, then, is a complete analysis of *Winnie-the-Pooh*. I believe serenely that no refutative elenchus (to borrow Professor McKeon's elegant term) would be capable of invalidating the series of propositions we have presented. It would be a grave mistake, if not indeed an out-and-out *hamartia*, for anyone to attempt this, for such a person would be pitting his individual critical talents against the authority of all the most disciplined and differentiated insights of antiquity and the Middle Ages. It is only by remaining loyal to our humanistic tradition of scientific poetics that we may do full justice to our literary texts and protect ourselves from that dehumanization of poetry that Professor Crane quite properly finds in the works of the "New Critics." We must ever keep in mind the admonition of Professor Maclean that the highest art (he was speaking of tragedy, but the point may be generalized) "has three dimensions, like anything with depth." [17] This brilliant principle—which, by the way, seems to me to apply to physics and solid geometry no less than to poetry—has not been altogether uninfluential in the determination of our methodological approach to

17 Maclean, *ibid.*, p. 608.

Winnie-the-Pooh, and if we have achieved some small degree of success in our structural analysis, I should like the credit to devolve upon soundness of method rather than on any particular merit in the acuity of the writer.

QUESTIONS AND STUDY PROJECTS

1. Professor Penwiper's treatment of the concept, "magnitude," is certainly among the most penetrating aspects of his essay. What, in your opinion, would be the proper magnitude to produce beauty in the genre of the essay? To arrive at the answer, be sure to conceive what would be too much magnitude and what would be not quite enough. Your desired figure should, if you have calculated correctly, lie roughly between these limits.

2. Choose a paragraph of *Pooh* that superlatively illustrates Professor Penwiper's useful definition of poetry: whole meaningful structures composed of the building blocks of language and the glue of experience. In order to capture the very essence of Milne's creative method, make two lists indicating which elements in the paragraph are the blocks and which the glue.

SIMON LACEROUS

*is perhaps the most feared and respected critic in England.
An implacable foe of sentimentality, flabby aestheticism,
and inflated reputations, he has made English authors
tremble since the publication of his first volume,* Assassina-
tions, *thirty years ago. Though he is a Fellow of Mag-
dalen College, Oxford, he despises the entire English
University system. Of his fellow Fellows he has said:
"They can all go to hell. Of course, some should go
before others. One has a responsibility to make discriminations." He and his wife, Trixie, were the guiding spirits
behind the now defunct but extremely influential quar-
terly,* Thumbscrew. *Several of the younger critics who
have taken up the battle against sentimentality, flabby
aestheticism, and inflated reputations owe their start and
their moral guidance to Dr. Lacerous.*

Another Book to Cross Off Your List

BY

SIMON LACEROUS

THE great English novels are *Sons and Lovers*, *Lady Chatterley's Lover*, and *Women in Love*. Some malicious persons, who have had the cheek to call me narrow-minded in the past, will doubtless welcome this statement as proof of their views. I don't care; I let it stick. There will always be literary scum to laugh at every honest effort to make tasteful discriminations, and we are now in greater need than ever before of critics—or shall I say, of *a* critic—who will stand up as a moral and aesthetic guide, leading the culture-hungry masses to the finest and purest literature and keeping the rest in outer darkness. If destiny must choose me as its messenger, I do not shirk from the call, but cry out in all directions: Beware, you complacent dolts who are still wallowing in Victorian trash! Beware, you academic leeches who will praise any dull sonnet you can find that has not already been worked over by your brethren! A judgment day is at hand! You are going to have to submit your crackpot notions and juvenile tastes to the severe gaze of common sense, intelligence, and Life!

D. H. Lawrence is the only English novelist worth reading. Now, I know that some of you—the sort that creep around in libraries looking for inconsistencies in a man's work—will say that my position has changed since last year, when I said the great English novelists were Richardson, Fanny Burney, Disraeli, and Lawrence. What you don't seem to realize is that in the meantime another book on the English novel has appeared, by Lord Wendell Dovetail. Now, Lord Wendell Dovetail is a fine person, I suppose; at least he has many friends in his circle, so I am told by some friends of mine who have some contacts in his circle (that kind of counterspy work is not for me, by the bye). I have nothing against Lord Wendell Dovetail personally. But really, I cannot be expected to keep my temper when he publishes a book saying that the great English novelists are Richardson, Fanny Burney, and Disraeli! I went out at once and reread these people, and so did Trixie, and we agreed that they were no good at all.

Now that I have gotten down to Lawrence alone, the number of English novelists on my Index is greater than ever, and this I take to be a sign that things may be improving at last on the literary scene. Perhaps readers are finally beginning to learn that their reading time is precious and very limited, and mustn't be wasted on third-raters like Fielding and Joyce.[1] There was an under-

---

1 Naturally, there are still persons willing to read into *Tom Jones* a few pages and then pretend to have devoured all of Fiel-

graduate just last week asking me which of Shakespeare's plays he should start with, to work up Shakespeare for his examinations. "Shakespeare!" I said. "Why, man, you haven't even read *The Rainbow* yet! Don't talk to me of Shakespeare until you've gone through Lawrence twice and made a list of everything he has to say against the Establishment." He took it rather hard, but the point is, he took it. Another soul saved from dilettantism, if I may put it thus.

Scarcely had I penned these last words when today's post arrived, and what should I find but a symposium in *The Listener* on *Winnie-the-Pooh*. With a sense of deep grievance I read through the various pieces, and, just as my misgivings foretold, it was true that every critic, while pretending to praise A. A. Milne, was in reality attacking me! Pages and pages of vile invective, so base and dastardly that the perpetrators dared not mention me by name or even allude to any of my work! Those of you who are outside the academic world can have no idea of the cowardice practiced by these "aesthetic" dons who will turn on everything honest and generous but will never expose themselves to censure by revealing that they are all in league against me. Well, they leave me no alternative but to say a few words about their latest idol.

The trouble with *Winnie-the-Pooh* is that it constitutes a vast betrayal of Life. This is simply put, and if I were merely addressing the loyal old *Thumbscrew* group, I would end my critique here. Unfortunately, there are

---

ding with hearty pleasure. The fact is, that when I get such people into my chambers, give them a straight look, and *demand* the *truth*, they admit to having aped the taste of several critics who bear me particular ill will. As for Joyce, he is a nasty trifler and, what is worse, an Irishman.

enemies as well as friends among my readers, and they need to be reminded what the absolute canons of taste consist of.[2] Literature must reflect, conform to, and serve the interests of Life; that is the point in a nutshell. This is to say that it must be *about* Life, it must be lifelike (i.e., no decadent "artiness" or "pure intellection"), and it must help to smash the Establishment. Perfectly simple, perfectly objective tools of judgment, yet very few persons have attempted to wield them, much less with the efficiency and devastation you will see below.

A vast betrayal of Life, then. It is only proper to say that everything Milne wrote, from his syrupy panegyric on the changing of guard at Buckingham Palace onwards, is a vast betrayal of Life. For minds with mature interests, however—and by mature interests I assure you I don't mean those of Clive Bell, Norman Douglas, and Lord Wendell Dovetail—there must be a special repugnancy in *Winnie-the-Pooh* and *The House at Pooh Corner*. They stand out so pompously, so flatulently, for the status quo; they are so lacking in moral seriousness. For someone like Lord Wendell Dovetail, of course, moral seriousness is a drawback. No doubt when you have been born to the purple and never had to do a day's honest work, you prefer worshipping frivolousness to facing the eternal moral questions that Cromwell and D. H. Lawrence faced, in their slightly different ways to be sure. Moral seriousness is demanded of us by Life; and the *Pooh* books, like all English fiction with the exception of *Sons and Lovers*, *Lady Chatterley's Lover*, and *Women in Love*, fail grossly and miserably to be morally serious enough for me.

2 For a fuller treatment see Trixie Lacerous, "The Absolute Canons of Taste," *Thumbscrew*, IV (1936). See also my review of this article in the same number.

To descend to specifics, I have just checked through *Sons and Lovers* again to verify my idea, and it is true that there is not a single element in *Winnie-the-Pooh* that touches upon real Life. Not one character is from the Midlands; not one is of working-class origin; and there is not even a coal mine on the ideal landscape where they jump and play. Do not mistake me for one of those vipers, the Marxists, who turn literature upside down to shake the social doctrine out of it. My interest is in the art of the novel; simply, there is no art without Life, and no Life without Midland coal mines. You see that I do not involve myself in supersubtle formulations that everyone must admire because no one understands them; I state the truth with hard simplicity, and it is this, I suppose, that rankles in the breasts of those who are hiding from Life.

Some readers, no doubt, have approached *Winnie-the-Pooh* hopefully, having heard that it dealt with a bear. Bears, after all, can be fierce and passionate, and this, combined with moral seriousness, is the very essence of Life. (It is to be regretted that Lawrence never gave us a bear-baiting scene to match his superb bullfight in *The*

Plumed Serpent.) What a shock, then, to find that our present hero is "Pooh Bear, Winnie-the-Pooh, F.O.P. (Friend of Piglet's), R.C. (Rabbit's Companion), P.D. (Pole Discoverer), E.C. and T.F. (Eeyore's Comforter and Tail-finder)." I do not believe there is a flabbier series of phrases in English literature! This Sir Edward Bear, Sir Pooh de Bear, is the very image of a fat old Tory who passes all his time pampering his depraved tastes and reminiscing about his imaginary exploits. Substitute port and brandy for condensed milk and honey, and you will recognize the likeness at once. He is a *flabby* bear, and flabbiness in literature is the thing I detest above all else. Lord Wendell Dovetail is flabby too, but let that pass; even he cannot match the slothfulness incarnate that goes by the name of "Pooh Bear" and is held up for our admiration by his namby-pamby creator.

Now, let us touch upon the question of moral seriousness. A work of fiction should, I believe, inculcate sound moral values (hatred of the Establishment) by seeing to it that the deserving characters crush the undeserving ones —or, in more concrete terms, that the vital, potent, incorruptibly moral lower-class characters, like the gamekeeper in *Lady Chatterley's Lover*, get the better of the effeminate leisure-class characters, like the cringing Chatterley.[3] It is not hard to see that, with these absolute canons of taste in mind, we must give *Pooh* a zero for moral seriousness. Quite simply, there *are* no deserving characters, and there's an end to the matter! This is not to say, of course,

---

3 If the reader cares to regard this sentence as being applicable to Life as well as literature, and inserts "Lacerous" and "Lord Wendell Dovetail" for the gamekeeper and Chatterley, I have no objection. But I do not care to digress onto personalities here; I am working on another little sketch of Lord Wendell Dovetail that will appear separately.

that Milne neglects to inculcate values; he simply rein-
forces all the wrong ones. The degenerate Pooh turns out
to be always right, while the two characters who most
nearly approach the level of human decency are con-
sistently rejected and mocked. I refer to Tigger, whose
healthy habit of bouncing upon the others by surprise is
frowned upon prudishly; and Eeyore, who suffers everyone's insults and neglect with never a flicker of sympathy
from the author. Milne's preference is obviously for the
more "normal" Pooh and Piglet, who are surrounded by
friends and never feel the moral necessity to lash out at
injustice the way Tigger, Eeyore, and I do.

Another absolute canon of taste is that literature be
lifelike. Though an author should arrange his plot to have
it resemble one of Lawrence's as exactly as possible, he
should never vary one inch from a mimetic reproduction
of the exact quality of Life as it is really and truly lived by
real people who are genuinely alive. Now, I have already
explained that this means coal-mining in the Midlands or
nothing. But *Winnie-the-Pooh* sins against lifelikeness
much more deeply than other non-carboniferous novels.
Its characters are not only unlifelike, they are protected
from every minutest contact with Life by the misplaced
ingenuity of A. A. Milne. At the very outset, when Sir
Pooh de Bear is in danger of floating up and out of the
special Establishment Forest where he and Christopher
Robin fritter away their days, Milne sees to it that the
balloon goes only to the treetops; when Pooh returns to
earth he has learned nothing whatever of educational
value about reality. Whether Pooh and Piglet are endangered by a flood or pretending to prepare themselves for
the attack of a wild beast, the atmosphere of placid tri-
fling is always smoothly preserved. Indeed, there is no

such thing as death in the world of Pooh.[4] When Baby Roo is being swept down a stream there are no serious thoughts of drowning, and when Owl's house crashes to the ground with great force, it is only the occasion for some lame humor as to which wall is now the ceiling. "Joke, Ha ha!" as Eeyore would say. It is all very, very funny, at least for those whose acquaintance with Life is so slight that they can imagine this to be real, sincere, morally responsible stuff.

"*Sed Musa hujus fabulae A. A. Milnei nec rustica nec urbana, sed suburbana.*"[5] This is the only intelligent comment that has been made about *Winnie-the-Pooh* outside my immediate family (and significantly, it was written neither by an Englishman nor in the English language). *Suburbana* is right! The point is that *Pooh* is nothing more nor less than a fictionalized training manual for Christopher Robin's entrance into the stuffy upper-bourgeois Establishment world. It's neither a country story nor a city story, but a complete *Cortegiano* for the smug little public-school boy. This, by the way, is the whole rationale of the plot, and since no one has so much as mentioned this self-evident fact in print, I suppose it falls to me to explain how the book should be read—or how the book might possibly have been read, with a minimum of moral damage to the reader, before I placed it on my Index.

The whole key to *Winnie-the-Pooh* is contained in the fact that A. A. Milne is hoping to intimidate and cajole his son out of his "childish ways," that is, out of the few

4 Here again the example of Lawrence makes us blush with shame for Milne's wishy-washiness. See Trixie Lacerous, "Bloody Death in the Works of D. H. Lawrence," *Thumbscrew*, III (1935), and my editorial comment in the same number.

5 Robertus Tracy, "Ursus Minor, or, The Bear as Swain," *Carleton Miscellany*, II (Summer, 1961), 118.

half-formed resistances in his character against Establishment little-boy values. Any doubts about this theory that one might entertain in reading *Winnie-the-Pooh* are swept away by *The House at Pooh Corner*, which positively wrenches Christopher's teddy bear away from him at the end and marches him off to school. The intimidation comes through very plainly in Milne's so-called "Contradiction," his excuse for an Introduction to the volume:

Why we are having a Contradiction is because last week when Christopher Robin said to me, "What about that story you were going to tell me about what happened to Pooh when—" I happened to say very quickly, "What about nine times a hundred and seven?" And when we had done that one, we had one about cows going through a gate at two a minute, and there are three hundred in the field, so how many are left after an hour and a half? We find these very exciting, and when we have been excited quite enough, we curl up and go to sleep. . . .

The clause, "We find these very exciting," ranks with some of Lord Wendell Dovetail's latest mouthings as one of the most hypocritical remarks of all time. "We" means A. A. Milne, of course, imposing his will on the poor boy, who in turn communicates an unintentional irony to the reader by falling asleep instead of doing his sums.

It thus appears that while Milne is superficially telling stories to amuse Christopher Robin, he is really "edifying" him, i.e. weaning him from his childhood by imperceptible stages. When even the staunch anti-intellectual Eeyore is found one day attempting to take up spelling, it is clear that Milne's invasion of the nursery will be ruthless, and so it is.[6] His coyest tricks of style are turned on:

6 Piglet's immediate reaction is the correct one. Seeing the spelling sticks laid out on the ground, he "thought that perhaps it was a Trap of some kind."

By the time it came to the edge of the Forest the stream had grown up, so that it was almost a river, and, being grown-up, it did not run and jump and sparkle along as it used to do when it was younger, but moved more slowly. For it knew now where it was going, and it said to itself, "There is no hurry. We shall get there some day." But all the little streams higher up in the Forest went this way and that, quickly, eagerly, having so much to find out before it was too late.

The message here is that it is time to give up your Lawrentian freedom and spontaneity, your full life of the senses and your natural childish interest in the world, and begin to roll along like a regular Colonel Blimp. I would almost prefer to read *frank* nonsense, *frank* idiocy like that of Sir Max Beerbohm or Ronald Firbank, than solemn "educational" nonsense like this.

Of course the most revolting part of it all has not yet been told. It is apparently not enough that Milne try to impose his Establishment values on Christopher Robin; he must see to it that Christopher Robin absorb the lesson so well as to become a hypocrite himself with regard to Pooh. Pooh is certainly no model of character, but he does have the one virtue, shared by many other Tories by the bye, of complete ingenuousness. This is precisely what Christopher Robin himself is in the process of unlearning, and as he becomes increasingly devious and discriminatory he becomes correspondingly cool to Pooh. Thus when Pooh offers the opinion that everyone in the world "is all right, *really*," Christopher Robin concurs with false heartiness, and shortly thereafter begins cutting Pooh himself. When he finally "goes away," i.e. heads off for Eton or Harrow I suppose, he does so in the best public-school style, not even informing his ex-companions of what he is up to. Pooh, the poor Falstaff to this methodical Hal, is bought off with an illusory knighthood and told to be understanding, "*whatever* happens." The reader may fill in the "*whatever*" for himself.

This, then, is the essential *Winnie-the-Pooh*, a book which violates the absolute canons of taste as flagrantly as any critic could desire. It is a book which, having brought its plot to a thoroughly disgusting end, must yet add an extra false note, a sickly last paragraph about a little boy and his bear playing "eternally" in an "enchanted" spot in a non-existent Forest. While Milne is making this saccharine exit, supposedly leaving you to dry a tear over Pooh and his ex-friend, we can picture all too easily what is really happening. Christopher Robin is being spruced up, fitted for his revolting little public-school uniform, and drilled in all the "graces" of the would-be aristocracy. From what I have inferred about Christopher Robin, indeed, I would imagine that he has by now grown up into a perfect prig, an enemy of everything that is decent, alive, and morally serious. The more I think about it, the more convinced I become that Christopher Robin not only hates everything I stand for, he hates me personally. Hates and despises my selfless efforts to bring culture to the masses! Come out, Christopher Robin, wherever you are hiding, and tell me to my face that you loathe me! I can take it, and, if the necessity so arises, I shall bring myself to say a few modest words in reply!

QUESTIONS AND STUDY PROJECTS

1. Read *Lady Chatterley's Lover* to understand more clearly Lacerous's absolute canons of taste. What strategies does *Lady Chatterley's Lover* provide us with for dealing with what situations? How does it equip us for Life?

2. The very existence of this Casebook would appear to cast some doubt—would it not?—on Lacerous's opinion that *Pooh* does not merit serious interest. Like the casebooks now devoted to *Catcher in the Rye* and to Mark Twain's Wound, this one constitutes a monument of general critical esteem for its subject. Discuss.

BENJAMIN THUMB,

Assistant Professor Emeritus at Oregon State, has never intruded himself into the "center ring" of the "scholarly circus," but his work is respected by a small, discriminating group of readers. He has long been a faithful contributor and—what is perhaps equally admirable—a steady subscriber, to Notes and Queries, *in which the present article was published.*

At his retirement dinner last year Professor Thumb was presented with a plaque, signed by seven of his colleagues, testifying to his forty years of loyal service to the University. The elegiac note at the end of the piece we reprint here may be accounted for by the fact that Professor Thumb intends to make no further contributions to scholarship, but to pass his remaining days visiting with his grandchildren and caring for his garden.

The Style of *Pooh:*
Sources, Analogues, and
Influences

BY

BENJAMIN THUMB

IN THE veritable pageant of literary criticism of *Winnie-the-Pooh* that we have lately witnessed, few authorities if any, I believe, have addressed themselves to the major questions that must, I submit, be asked about any work of art. These are, what are the work's literary sources, what works does it closely resemble, and what subsequent works has it influenced? Without full information on these points there would seem, I confess, to be little hope of reaching adequate critical conclusions as to the work's scope, meaning, and value. If, for example, someone had not discovered that *King Lear* owes its origin and many of its details to Geoffrey of Monmouth's *Historia Regum Britanniae,* the wealth of marvelous present-day comment on that play would have been rendered impossible. That everyone is now in perfect agree-

ment over the meaning of *Lear* is attributable directly to
the concurrence of opinion over the fact that Shakespeare
was, truly and indeed, following Geoffrey of Monmouth.
At the same time, once this crucial point was settled, it
was a simple matter for commentators to decide why
Shakespeare made his few "improvements," or at any
rate alterations, upon Geoffrey's story. Nor, blessedly, is
there any shortage of studies of analogues and influences
in Shakespeare's case. How saddening, then, to turn to
Winnie-the-Pooh, a work scarcely inferior in its own
genre to *King Lear*, only to discover that the barest be-
ginnings have yet to be made. The field of sources, analogues, and influences is so broad as to be nearly intimi-
dating, and the reader will pardon me for undertaking in
this article only one rather narrow, albeit important,
facet of the subject, namely, the sources, analogues, and
influences of *Pooh*'s style.

The wary hunter for sources will always profit from
considering the year in which the work in question was
published; for, if a suspected source is found to postdate
it, there is good reason to suspect that we are dealing not
with a source but with an influence. And, further, if the
two works were issued in the same year and there seems
to be no way of determining which one influenced the
other, we are rescued by the handy concept of the analogue; the two books are simply analogous, each to the
other. Of course the range of possible analogues is not
restricted to cases like this, which are really quite special;
but it is well to keep the theoretical possibilities of one's
work in mind from the beginning, to comfort one if any
particularly severe problems arise.

In the case of *Winnie-the-Pooh*, a consideration of the
date (1926) actually leads us to the first clue as to the

sources of its style. The book was written, we recall, at the height of the (rather unfortunate, in my opinion) modern revolution against the style and taste of Victorian poetry. Hulme, Eliot, and Pound had already spoken up in favor of more "difficult," more "classical," more "concrete" verse, and the style of modern practitioners, including Eliot and Pound, had pointed the way for other poets who were not content with the quite taxing difficulties of *Sordello* and the *Idylls of the King*, but had to go back to Donne, Herbert, and Crashaw for deeper obscurities. Thus we may justly expect *Winnie-the-Pooh*, as a product of this era, to show some "Metaphysical" traits of style. The whole book, indeed, is shot-through with this influence. In the interest of saving space in this journal, which I know is crammed with important articles, I shall content myself with a single example. "Once upon a time, a very long time ago now, about last Friday . . ." says Milne in the opening chapter. This is suspiciously near to Donne's

> *Now thou hast lov'd me one whole day,*
> *To morrow when thou leav'st, what wilt thou say?*

Now, though it is true that the Metaphysicals have momentarily driven the Victorians out of fashion, there is one author whose stock continues to rise as the years go by, and that is Shakespeare. As the year 1926 was no exception to this rule, we are not surprised to find echoes of the Sweet Singer of Avon virtually everywhere in *Pooh*. Again I must give only a single indication of this pervasive borrowing. Here is a passage from the famous chapter introducing Kanga and Roo:

"You ought to look at that tree right over there," said Rabbit. . . .

"I can see a bird in it from here," said Pooh. "Or is it a fish?"

"You ought to see that bird from here," said Rabbit. "Unless it's a fish."

"It isn't a fish, it's a bird," said Piglet.

"So it is," said Rabbit.

"Is it a starling or a blackbird?" said Pooh.

"That's the whole question," said Rabbit. "Is it a blackbird or a starling?"

I feel very sorry for any reader who might be so ignorant as to fail to recognize this exchange as a replica of Hamlet's "Very like a whale" conversation with Polonius.

Next, it would be rather astonishing if *Winnie-the-Pooh* turned out to have absorbed no influences from works of prose fiction, since it falls into that very category itself. Sure enough, quite early in *Pooh* we find extremely strong reminiscences of one of the great masters of modern prose fiction. Here is Pooh speaking: "It is either Two Woozles and one, as it might be, Wizzle, or Two, as it might be, Wizzles and one, if so it is, Woozle." This follows the syntax of Henry James, and is every bit as meaningful as one of James's later sentences, I feel. Nor does the influence end here. Let us pick at random a dialogue from *The House at Pooh Corner*:

"Well?" said Rabbit.

"Yes," said Owl, looking Wise and Thoughtful. "I see what you mean. Undoubtedly."

"Well?"

"Exactly," said Owl. "Precisely." And he added, after a little thought, "If you had not come to me, I should have come to you."

"Why?" asked Rabbit.

"For that very reason," said Owl, hoping that something helpful would happen soon.

"Yesterday morning," said Rabbit solemnly, "I went to see Christopher Robin. He was out. Pinned on his door was a notice!"

"The same notice?"

"A different one. But the meaning was the same. It's very odd."

"Amazing," said Owl, looking at the notice again, and getting, just for a moment, a curious sort of feeling that something had happened to Christopher Robin's back. "What did you do?"

"Nothing."

"The best thing," said Owl wisely.

"Well?" said Rabbit again, as Owl knew he was going to.

"Exactly," said Owl.

For a little while he couldn't think of anything more; and then, all of a sudden, he had an idea.

"Tell me, Rabbit," he said, "the *exact* words of the first notice. This is very important. Everything depends on this. The *exact* words of the *first* notice."

"It was just the same as that one really."

. . . "The exact words, please," he said, as if Rabbit hadn't spoken.

"It just said, 'Gone out. Backson.' Same as this, only this says 'Bisy Backson' too."

Owl gave a great sigh of relief.

"Ah!" said Owl. "*Now* we know where we are."

Compare this with the Old Artificer:

But he had also again questions and stops—all as for the mystery and the charm. "You looked it up—without my having asked you?"

"Ah, my dear," she laughed, "I've seen you with Bradshaw! It takes Anglo-Saxon blood."

" 'Blood'?" he echoed. "You've that of every race!" It kept her before him. "You're terrible."

Well, he could put it as he liked. "I know the name of the inn."

"What is it then?"

"There are two—you'll see. But I've chosen the right one. And I think I remember the tomb," she smiled.

"Oh, the tomb—!" Any tomb would do for him. "But I mean I had been keeping my idea so cleverly for you, while there you already were with it."

"You had been keeping it 'for' me as much as you like. But how do you make out," she asked, "that you were keeping it *from* me?"

"I don't—now. How shall I ever keep anything—some day when I shall wish to?"

"Ah, for things I mayn't want to know, I promise you shall find me stupid." They had reached their door, where she herself paused to explain. "These days, yesterday, last night, this morning, I've wanted everything."

Well, it was all right. "You shall have everything." [1]

The virtual identity of narrative manner between these two passages is made the more convincing by the disparity of subject matter treated. For while Milne is giving us a debate over the meaning of a written notice, James is rendering a torrid love scene between two experienced adulterers. There is, I believe, little to choose between the two for sheer dramatic quality.

So much for the sources of *Winnie-the-Pooh*'s style; we must now search for analogues and influences. We can find both, luckily enough, in the same spot if we merely consider the outstanding feature of style in the book. This is, of course, Milne's knack of coining nonsense-words in accordance with his characters' difficulties in spelling, pronunciation, and experience of the world. When Pooh mistakes an ambush for a gorse-bush, when the North Pole is imagined to be a stick, and when "Happy Birthday" comes out "HIPY PAPY BTHUTHDTH THUTHDA BTHUTHDY," we know that there is only one writer to whom we can turn: James Joyce. Now, I personally would have been content if that difficult gentleman had never been born; in his hands we can scarcely recognize the smooth English tongue we had learned to love in Edmund Gosse, Walter Besant, and G. K. Chesterton. As scholars, however, we have a duty to consider all influences objectively, and the sad fact is that Joyce has been both influenced and influential. Whether he should fall under the heading of analogue or influence in the present case is somewhat debatable, as *Ulysses* came before *Winnie-the-Pooh* and *Finnegans Wake* after. I cannot, in good conscience, seriously propose to myself the possibility that Milne may have read Joyce; surely his imagination was ever too pure to take nourishment from the compost heap. But since deep similarities exist in word play, I think a reasonable compromise would be to say that *Pooh* is analogous to *Ulysses* and is an influence upon *Finnegans Wake*. This, I trust, settles the matter, and we need only add a few more specific examples to show that the parallels are really there.

There is, first of all, Pooh's misconstruction of "customary procedure" as "Crustimoney Proseedcake," which is altogether worthy of H. C. Earwicker (if we must admire this sort of thing at all). There is Milne's "Contradiction" introducing *The House at Pooh Corner*—the exact source, I believe, of Joyce's term "Exagmination" in discussing the unfinished *Work in Progress* (or *Finnegans Wake*). And one final example, chosen quite at random, is Piglet's series of cries, "Help, help, a Herrible Hoffalump! Huff, Huff, a Hellible Horralump!" and so on. Beyond any doubt, this is the original of Joyce's notorious: "And ho! Hey? What all men? Hot? His tittering daughters of. Whawk?"

Limitations of space will prevent further sampling of parallels at this time, but the reader, having seen that it can be done, may be encouraged to disinter further sources, analogues, and influences on his own. As for myself, my long lifetime of writing notes, answering queries, submitting answers to others' queries, and submitting queries to others' notes, is drawing to a close at last. I shall feel that my time has not been altogether misspent if, in the next few numbers of this journal, we can see a real old-fashioned controversy arising over *Winnie-the-Pooh,* with such titles as "The *Real* Sources of *Winnie-the-Pooh*" and "Crustimoney Proseedcake Once More" contending for authority as the final word. It is, after all, in such vital interplay of scholarly minds and wits that the truth about literature eventually gets told; my own modest function has been, at the best, to uncover here an analogue, there an influence, and to stimulate the minds of other and perhaps better scholars to continue the work that I have had the initiative to begin, but not, alas! the time to finish.

QUESTIONS AND STUDY PROJECTS

1. Professor Thumb makes allusion to the general critical agreement now happily prevailing on the subject of *King Lear*, a play by Shakespeare. Get your teacher to recommend two or three articles on *Lear* from one of the many Shakespeare casebooks; read the articles, and make a report to your class on the agreed-upon meaning of the play. If you find that you have some extra time, you might read *King Lear* itself.

2. Who was James Joyce? Do you agree with the wish that he had never been born, or do you subscribe rather to a "live and let live" philosophy?

KARL ANSCHAUUNG, M.D.,

one of the last survivors of Freud's original circle of Viennese followers in the first decade of this century, died in 1960 after an extremely active career as an analyst. In an autobiographical memoir written just before the end, he declared that "I have never swerved one inch from the basic teachings of Freud. Never, never, never. Not one inch. I have remained faithful to Freud through thick and thin. That is the justification of all my work." In the last years of his life Dr. Anschauung turned his attention to literary problems, "in the hope," he wrote, "of clearing up one or two matters on which the Master left us incomplete formulations." One happy result was the following article, here reprinted from the journal Lustprinzip *and translated into English by Dr. B. B. Braille. Dr. Braille, incidentally, wants your editor to mention that he was among the first and best translators of Freud, and commends your attention especially to the original jokes he substituted for Freud's in translating* Wit and Its Relation to the Unconscious.*

A. A. Milne's
Honey-Balloon-Pit-Gun-Tail-Bathtubcomplex

BY

KARL ANSCHAUUNG, M.D.

THERE is often heard the opinion that psychoanalysis is unfriendly to literature, that we regard the artist as a neurotic, that writing is a for us quite antithetical to the Reality Principle activity. What is uncanny [*unheimlich*] [1] is that I have often felt this to be true myself. Uncanny I nevertheless say, inasmuch as we who have remained faithful to Freud realize consciously that he was always friendly to art. In his writings find we, it is true, various opinions at various stages of his progress toward a unified field theory of the arts; but although he died untimely before this ultimate together-gathering could be expressed for us, we can see its main outlines sufficiently well to understand the progressive trend of

[1] I have reproduced the original German wherever there has been any doubt about shadings of meaning.—Trans.

thought which he from the beginning was on. We can now affirm, that at no time did Freud mean seriously to imply that the artist was from other men fully divided by his away-turning from the Reality Principle. True, the artist must be regarded as a Narcissist regrettably unable to overcome regressive tendencies fixating his libido at pre-Oedipal cathexes, and hence [*also*] seeking in masturbatory phantasy-play an outletting of repressed materials which he upon the unsuspecting public wishes to impose in the secondarily elaborated form of "art." So much, no one would now deny. But as Freud gathered ever more weighty evidence from his studies, he gradually realized, that such aetiology not solely to artists, but to everyone applied—doctor, lawyer, Indian chief—and that the artist was, if anything, better off than, let us say, the statesman who, as a result of persisting interest in infantile theories of anal birth, must send flights of bombers over other countries and keep himself unusually clean and fastidious. As for my uncanny feeling that Freud denigrated art, in self-analysis I have repressed materials discovered, suggesting this to be a residue of unresolved envy of the Master dating from our first meeting in 1906 when I upon the floor passed out cold.

False then it is, to assert, that Freud with anything but sincerest respect regarded artists and writers. He was always quite clear on the point, that the artist *as artist* [*a l s K ü n s t l e r*] was not especially neurotic, was indeed directly prevented by his art from being as neurotic as the normal man on the street. For the demands which the Reality Principle makes upon all of us, no one is entirely prepared; lucky then is he who a Pleasure Principle outlet can find, which re-attaches him to reality by earning him honor, power, riches, fame, and the love of women. Precisely such a case is the present patient, A. A. Milne. Of neurotic features in his social character he has displayed little signs, beyond to be sure the customary psychopathology of everyday life. For this reason the tireless researcher is encouraged to out-seek in his art, those perversions, phobias, incipient psychoses, fixations, sublimations, phantasies, and phylogenetic traces, which would have formed his character had he taken up some other line of work. It is an ontological problem, and not one for our strictly scientific studies, to decide whether such information, taken together, may be called the A. A. Milne's-character or must be relegated to the realm of might-have-been. For my part, I am to the former view inclined, by recalling that no such scruples prevented Jones from explaining Shakespeare's incestuous designs on his mother, nor Ferenczi from discovering Swift's im-potence-anxiety-determined distaste for very large girls, nor the Master himself from revealing Leonardo's early relations with a vulture.

Foremost among the problems offered us by *Winnie-the-Pooh* and *The House at the Corner of Pooh's* [*Das Haus bei der Poohecke*], we may place the question, what is Milne's unconscious attitude to bears? The frequent presence on the illusionistic phantasy-screen, or "plot," of these two books, of a bear, strongly points to an ob-sessive nosology, the which, in fact, is fully in an examina-tion of Milne's poetry borne out. Examine if you please a poem written in early childhood (hence the volume's title *As We Extremely Young Were*), "Lines and Squares":

Whenever I walk in a London street,
I'm ever so careful to watch my feet;
*   And I keep in the squares,*
*   And the masses of bears,*

Who wait at the corners all ready to eat
The sillies who tread on the lines of the street,
  Go back to their lairs,
  And I say to them, "Bears,
  Just look how I'm walking in all of the squares!" [usw.]

Here have we a classic infantile phobia not dissimilar to that of the by-Freud-treated little Hans. Milne imagines, that he is on all sides endangered by dreadful bears who will, unless he performs an obsessive ritual essentially similar to those of the Christian Church, attack and devour him. That the suckling babe A. A. Milne found it impossible, to off-shake his phobia in the immediately-following years, we demonstrate with these lines written at age six:

  Round *about*
  And round *about*
  And round *about I go;*
  I think I am a Traveller escaping from a Bear.

From these early phantasies we draw the plain connection, that *Winnie-the-Pooh* from a defensive reaction mechanism stems, employing the projective technique of inversion of affect: the feared bear becomes the loved bear, the enemy becomes the inseparable-friend. Thus in daydream the severely phobic A. A. Milne makes a pathetic, clinically most interesting attempt, discovered by me, to deny his phobia and rid himself of his obsessive-traits. This diagnosis, as well as explaining the anxiety reduction function of many chapters in the Milne's book,[2] offers a

2 For example: the second poetic fragment above leads us to expect, that somewhere in *Winnie-the-Pooh* an episode will find itself, wherein A. A. Milne placidly stationary remains, while the feared but now fearful bear wanders around and around in a state of uncathected anxiety. Chapter Three, "In Which a Woozle Is by Hunting Pooh and Piglet Nearly Caught," is this case exactly.

general clue to further psycholiterary mysteries, as will below be seen.

Having shown that the phantasy-character, "Pooh," serves A. A. Milne the purpose, of his bear phobia temporarily to assuage by demanding an affectionate not a libido-inhibited anxiety-response, there remains us the more difficult task to discover what sequence of experiences led the infant A. A. Milne, to his bear phobia in the first place develop. Although Milne's "literary" work is for the purpose to *deny* his phobia intended, we may expect, that under the universal law of the return of the repressed, his repressed materials will of necessity themselves express [*sich aussprechen*] within the text. Of this our expectation the fulfillment is indeed speedy.[3] Before we have even properly at the beginning of the story arrived, find we, in Milne's "Introduction," this note:

So when Christopher Robin goes to the Zoo, he goes to where the Polar Bears are, and he whispers something to the third keeper from the left, and doors are unlocked, and we wander through dark passages and up steep stairs, until at last we come to the special cage, and the cage is opened, and out trots something brown and furry, and with a happy cry of "Oh, Bear!" Christopher Robin rushes into its arms.

Here have we, not merely a confirmation of the overcarry from Milne's poetically celebrated bear-phobia to his bear-character Pooh, but also an unmistakable representation of the underlying Pooh's meaning [*Urpoohdeu-*

3 Note for Teachers: From this point onward Dr. Anschauung's paper goes into subject matter that some students may find offensive. Teachers of coeducational classes may want to end one day's assignment at this sentence. Your editor has thought it best, however, nor to follow the confusing practice of some casebook compilers who prune their selections by too free a use of ellipses and résumés, which may arbitrarily maim the author's argument and unduly shorten the total length of the casebook.—Ed.

tung]. Freud's *Interpretation of Dreams* [4] shows us unequivocally, that to "wander through dark passages and up steep stairs" can only a coitus-equivalent signify. When further we arrive at the opening of a special cage and the out-trotting of something brown and furry, embraced by A. A. Milne, the reader may easily imagine, that all doubt ceases to retain validity. The friendly male bear Pooh is meant, the unfriendly terrifying female organ to represent.

It thus seems likely, that what, the which we have to deal with here, is a Primal Scene [5] witnessed by the infant A. A. Milne, overcharged with free-floating anxiety, and hence into the somewhat more manageable bear-phobia transposed, leading to formation of obsessive ritual meant to avoid to face situations calling for resurgence from the unconscious, past the doors of the preconscious, into the superego-dominated conscious mind of A. A. Milne's, of the repressed material. Thus much is perfectly obvious. There gives no reason to doubt, that all the classic Primal-Scene reactions were in this case present: the sadistic, and secondarily masochistic, misunderstanding of the Scene in terms of assault and battery, the hatred of the father as unique possessor of "Pooh Bear," generalized envy and impotence-anxiety resulting from small size of oneself, resentment of "unfaithful" mother, fear of abandonment, vicarious stimulation of racial memory-traces, and, of course, total repression and "forgetting" of the entire

4 Translated by Braille.—Trans.

5 Students will want to know the exact meaning of this term. A Primal Scene, as I understand it, is an event of great significance (according to the school of thought represented by this article) in the lives of some unlucky small children, who, because of cramped housing conditions, lower-class family habits, or mere chance, find themselves present during functions unsuitable for the healthy development of their imaginations.—Ed.

scene. (No piece of evidence is stronger, than the fact, that A. A. Milne never mentions this trauma to anyone.) [6] To critics whose interest is more strictly literary, and not psychoaliterary, I leave the work of to document these facts. More pressing in concern for us is the humanitarian task of trying to help A. A. Milne, his bear-phobia to overcome. This will require further and closer attention to a variety of superficially unconnected, actually quite strictly determined and related, elsewhere in the text symptoms.

Let us then upon a seemingly different investigation outset, and try some word-associations on the patient. Even C. G. Jung, before his unfortunate attack of insanity in 1912, got good results from this technique. The present disadvantage, of A. A. Milne's absence from my office, will not hamper us if we in mind keep the realization, that works of art are under conditions of relaxed superego censorship written, thus [also] yielding formerly repressed patterns almost as successfully, as private analytical sessions, lacking however the stimulating incentives of transference and very high fees. In A. A. Milne's "fictional" memoir *Winnie-the-Pooh* find we a complex of key words, the which points clearly to screen memories hiding the Primal Scene and us helping to exactly the sequence of infantile-experiences reconstruct.

Remembering that A. A. Milne has already been overexcitable proven by references to *pudendum mulieris*, let us propose to him the associations "pit" and "jar," both of course time-honored symbols of the same. To our amazement discover we that these very words are togetherjoined in the "plot" of *Winnie-the-Pooh*. A. A. Milne explains, in "Piglet a Heffalump Meets," that if he were to

6 I have written him several letters and no reply received.

attempt, someone to trap, he would do so by employing a
jar of honey and a large pit! That "honey" has itself a
genital-erotic significance, no one with a good English
language command can seriously deny. The inseparability
of "Pooh" and honey further cements this identification.
Thus have we a cluster, pit-jar-honey, of definite aetio-
logical significance in A. A. Milne's symptom-formation.
In this very Heffalump-chapter see we some consequences
of this. The Heffalump, whose masculine role so evident
is that it was by an ignorant layman noticed,[7] is to fall
headlong into the pit-jar-honey "trap"—an exact equivalent, need I hardly say, of the catastrophic Primal Scene
effect upon the impressionable tot A. A. Milne. The
infantile castration horror, invariable in these cases,
breaks past the superego in the thinly-disguised-form of
commentary upon honey jars. Thus the jar is a "something
mysterious, a shape and no more," and again "a great
enormous thing, like—like nothing. A huge big—well, like
a—I don't know—like an enormous big nothing." May I
point out, that the object inspiring this latter negativistic
definition is really Pooh him-or-herself, capped (with
redundant symbolism) by a honey jar?

If we now ask A. A. Milne, still harder to think about
jars, we bring up the following screen memory: the infant
A. A. Milne compulsively inserts and removes an ex-
balloon from an ex-honey jar, both presented to him by
two "others" on his "birthday." Here prove we the hypothesis of racial memory-trace stimulation, for tiny A. A.
Milne a dim awareness shows that copulation and childbirth (the birthday) are related. The destructive impression of the Primal Scene is, again, ingeniously by the

7 Myron Masterson, "Velenous Happy Land: Pooh's Chassis."
(See pp. 41–51, above.—Ed.)

unconscious represented in terms of burst balloon and emptied jar; while the mechanical, repetitive nature of A. A. Milne's act [8] points to the anxiety neurosis sufferer's obsessive re-enacting of the "others'" (Mummy and Daddy's) traumatic activity, in the hope of this time generating adequate ego-responses to cathect anxiety.

Our list of screen-associations now reads, pit-jar-honey-balloon. At once A. A. Milne the further association recalls, balloon-honey-gun. Upon investigation find we, that in the very first chapter of his most interesting memoir, A. A. Milne himself imagines as flying upward toward honey, aided by a balloon, and shot down by a gun. This is self-explanatory. On the wings of male potency—symbolized by the expanded balloon which characteristically "deflated" was by the Primal Scene—A. A. Milne hopes with infantile naïveté, the previously explained honey to seize. Instead he is discouraged and punished, by the agency of a gun, evidently representing the superior paternal phallus. It is now clear, that the A. A. Milne's-bear-phobia upon a solid base of impotence-anxiety resides. This is confirmed by the next association of "gun." "Coming to see me have my bath?" A. A. Milne recalls having asked his father immediately after the shooting, and when the father somewhat ambiguously answered, young Milne this question added: "I didn't hurt him when I shot him, did I?" The projection of himself into the maiming-father's-role here, altogether predictable was as a typical defense; much more interesting [*interes-*

---

8 This is not of course the only repetition-compulsion example in *Winnie-the-Pooh*, a book in which the Nirvana principle and the sadomasochistic complex also lavishly illustrated are. The force of Thanatos, perhaps nowhere better illustrated is, than in A. A. Milne's neurotic chanting, "Cottleston, Cottleston, Cottleston Pie," a bearing much further analysis hum.

santer] is the introduction of a new, exhibitionistic element in the neurosis. Having himself hallucinated into the personage of castrating imago, young Milne "worries" about the overefficiency of his organ in its intimidation of the father. He wants the father him to watch bathing, ostensibly for the purpose to reassure him that he (A. A. Milne) is still childlike. Yet at the same time, the experienced analyst cannot himself prevent, from seeing a more ego-syntonic motivation here. The screen-memory of being watched bathing by the father, surely a superego-distortion is, for *watching the father bathing*, the which in turn is, perfectly obviously, desired for the reason of reassuring oneself that the father really lacking is, in the terrifying physical power observed in the Primal Scene. A superficial and benevolent exhibitionism, in other words, a secondary elaboration for a malicious skoptophilia [9] is.

Skoptophilia, as the Master has taught us, is proper to the pre-genital organization of the libido, and specifically, to the anal-sadistic phase. Recalling the slang meaning of "Pooh," we see that the suckling A. A. Milne a further problem had—as yet unresolved—of confusing anal theories of childbirth with his memory of the Primal Scene. With this clue seek we among Milne's recollections a series of references to the erogenous zone in question. At once the final piece in our little puzzle, to us itself presents. A certain ass, A. A. Milne recalls, has *lost its tail*. The meaning of this missing object is never in doubt. Its owner extremely "attached to it" was; "it reminds me of something," says A. A. Milne; and "somebody must have taken it," adds he, echoing every child's feeling upon stumbling across the between boys and girls difference. Upon the re-attachment of this object, A. A. Milne so affected is,

9 This word is not in my dictionary.—Ed.

that he "came over all funny, and had to hurry home for
a little snack of something to sustain him." Now, this
rather complicated phantasy shows us, that A. A. Milne
still unconsciously some doubt retains, as to the basic
mechanical principles operative in the Primal Scene.
Whether intercourse is posterior or anterior, he evidently
cannot decide. Hence in his phantasy of helpful restora-
tion to the "wounded" mother, he to the mistaken side
wishes to re-attach the "tail." His motive for so doing is

divided, between (1) wish to ingratiate oneself with
mother by doing useful errand, (2) provide weapon
(along lines of sadistic misinterpretation of Scene) for
mother to counterattack and possibly slay father, (3)
demonstrate one's own ability to serve family harmony by
skillful manipulation of "tail," quite improbable in reality,
and (4) general tendency of small children not their own
business to be able to mind. That A. A. Milne himself
imagines, upon completion of this feat, a snack of honey
proceeding to devour, uncovers his absolutely basic,
underlying all else motive in this projection, namely a
most encouraging, perfectly healthy and normal Oedipal
plan, his mother to seduce.

This last feature leads us to believe, that A. A. Milne, if

he will present himself for treatment, an excellent chance stands of becoming out-straightened. His case is a relatively simple one of advanced animal-phobia and obsessional defense, somewhat complicated it is true by anal-sadistic and oral-helpful phantasies, skoptophilia and secondary exhibitionism, latently homosexual trends in identification with the mother, severe castration anxiety and compensatory assertiveness, and persistence of infantile misconstructions of birth, intercourse, and excretion. Doubtless when he appears in my office A. A. Milne further little symptoms will reveal, such as nail-biting, fascination with the analyst's foot, excessive squabbling over fees, and so on [*und so weiter*]. All these, Herr Milne, and others may to the surface be brought, and you may, as you in all likelihood wished to be in undertaking your confessions to write, become a healthy and useful member-of-society. Whatever therapeutic value you have achieved from your dirty linen before the general public airing, think how much more you will get from it presenting in a bundle to me. My deductive powers, plus your limitless ability, obscene and meaningful phantasies to regurgitate, might combine, many hundreds of happy and fruitful analytic hours to create for us both.

QUESTIONS AND STUDY PROJECTS

1. Are Anschauung's difficult technical terms always warranted, or would you sometimes prefer to see more familiar words in their place? Try to compose adequate substitutes wherever you can—for example, "affectionate" in place of "libidinal," "unsociable attitude" for "repression," and "temporary family disharmony" for "Oedipus Complex." Doesn't the argument of the essay become more appealing when such clarifications have been made?

2. Compare Anschauung's essay with Culpepper's Christian interpretation of *Pooh*. What is the relation of psychology to religion, religion to psychology, and both to literature? Must we conclude that life is relative, or absolute?

SMEDLEY FORCE,

editor of The Watermark *and Professor of English at the University of Texas, has long been an outstanding spokesman for what he calls "responsible criticism." "I am against irresponsibility in criticism," is the way he likes to phrase it. Your editor confesses that he feels a bias in favor of Professor Force's approach; critical fads may come and go, but here we have a genuine* scholar *who believes that new methods must prove their superiority to the tried and true ones before he will give them his (very influential) support. His editorials in* The Watermark *against irresponsible new trends have caused something of a mild sensation among the readers of that journal. Professor Force is the author of several books, including the popular* Checklist of Fauna and Flora in Pre-Romantic Literary Gardens *and the three-volume labor of love,* A Bibliographical Guide to Misquotations.

The present piece was read before an enthusiastic gathering of the Principles of Criticism Section of the Modern Language Association at the Annual Meeting, 1962. Your editor was privileged to be on hand and was thus enabled to record some of the audience's responses.

Prolegomena to Any
Future Study of
Winnie-the-Pooh

BY

SMEDLEY FORCE

L ET'S put a stop to the nonsense that's being written
about *Winnie-the-Pooh*! [Murmurs of approval.]
This is the fervent plea, gentlemen, that I should like to
place before your consideration this afternoon—a plea
from the heart of an "old-timer" who perhaps has seen
his day, but who cannot easily forget the standards of
Manly, Skeat, Kittredge, Chambers, and Greg. ["Hear,
hear!"] I can recall times when it was still conceivable
that a man might be both a scholar and, believe it or not,
yes, a gentleman! How different from these present days,
when on all sides we see swarms of industrious and in-
genious little graduate students—many of them, I must
say, looking as if they were scarcely off the boat from
Eastern Europe or worse—hatching, if I may phrase it
thus, hatching out of various suspect Ph.D. factories and

invading our universities with their "insights," their cant
about ironies and paradoxes, and their relentless desire to
see "symbolism" everywhere. How refreshing it is, after
my painful duties as reader for some of our more rep
utable journals, when I have passed a tiresome afternoon
mailing out rejection slips, to browse at will through some
real scholarship—to reread Klaeber's scrupulous, yet altogether charming and urbane footnotes to *Beowulf*, for
example. Klaeber! When comes such another, gentlemen?—to quote the poor Bard who has suffered the most
from the cheapening of our literary standards. When
we look about us today to see who is preparing to fill
such shoes as Klaeber's, what do we find? "Paradoxical
Persona: The Hierarchy of Heroism in *Winnie-the-Pooh*"
[laughter]; "Poisoned Paradise: The Underside of *Pooh*"!
[Laughter and groans.] The time has come for someone to
speak out against such rubbish; and this, gentlemen, is
why I dare to present myself before you this afternoon.[1]

Those of you who have followed my doubtless over-
long career will certainly not be quick to accuse me of
being an enemy to criticism. I have always maintained
that the proper criticism of literature is among the highest
activities the Lord has endowed us to perform. But you
will note, I am sure, that I said *proper* criticism. I cannot earnestly believe that we were intended to pass our
days hunting through the classics of our language for
symbols, corn-gods, and the like. Surely you will agree,
gentlemen, that criticism is only possible after certain
preliminary matters have been agreed upon. Having
screened all your applications for admission to this Sec-

1 This was said with characteristic and perhaps unnecessary
humility, as Professor Force happened to be the Chairman of the
MLA section he was addressing that day.—Ed.

tion, I know you understand that criticism must be postponed until the text has been definitively established, the *lacunae* surrounded (but not replaced) with a sufficiently broad range of conjectured readings, the variorum footnotes, appendices, bibliographies, and concordances fully compiled. When we turn from the current stream of drivel on *Winnie-the-Pooh* and ask ourselves how much of this indispensable groundwork for useful study of the book has been laid, we discover—what we of course suspected merely by virtue of having lived on into this decadent age—that nothing of merit has even been begun! I grant you that true criticism, strictly speaking, is not yet possible for *any* English author; I, certainly, at any rate, would not care to join the Babel of guesswork about the meaning of Shakespeare's plays until someone has given us a complete and accurate cardboard scale model of the Blackfriars Theatre. But the slickness, irrelevance, and Devil-may-care irresponsibility of Modern Criticism are nowhere more in evidence than in the case of *Winnie-the-Pooh*. What I aim to accomplish this afternoon (for, gentlemen, I assure you that I am not going to monopolize your precious time merely to be negative and cantankerous) is to set forth my idea of what needs to be done on this book; and to ask you, in your capacity as editors and dissertation advisers, to see to it that no further "Oedipus Complexes" and "mythopoeias" are allowed to slip into print until the foundations for mature criticism have been sunk irrefrangibly into the text of *Winnie-the-Pooh*.

Here, then, are some topics that will bear fruitful investigation, either by your distinguished selves or by your carefully supervised *protégés*. First, we must all be struck by the paucity of biographical connections between *Winnie-the-Pooh* and the lives of A. A. Milne,

"Christopher Robin," and the historical personages who probably lie behind the fictional portraits of "Pooh," "Piglet," "Kanga," *et alia*. A study in this vein might properly begin at the Dedication of the entire volume "To Her." True, this seems to refer to a member of Milne's family, perhaps even of his immediate family; but what a windfall it would be for some worthy scholar to reveal that it was really "another woman" in the author's life! [Hearty laughter.] Careers, gentlemen, entire careers have been built upon slighter discoveries than this. Less spectacular, no doubt, but equally of value to future criticism would be a thorough inquiry into the carry-over from the real "Christopher Robin," whom I assume to be a near acquaintance of the author's, to the "Christopher Robin" of storyland. How can we possibly attach any "significance" to the fictional Christopher's actions until we have first assured ourselves that they *are* fictional? If, for example, the child really had a teddy bear named "Pooh," the publication of this single fact could put an end to speculations about the so-called "relationship" between the two characters in the book. Pooh and Christopher Robin would simply be Pooh and Christopher Robin, and that would be that. You will find some remarks in Milne's *Autobiography* telling which characters he "invented" and which ones he took from stuffed animals, but I need not remind you that such statements in themselves do not constitute effective literary evidence. Perhaps Milne was telling less than the whole truth, and, if he wasn't, what does it mean to put a stuffed animal into literature? I believe it is self-evident that one would add to the "characters" of such prototypes with details from the lives of one's friends and enemies. Who, then, were *really* the officious Rabbit, the melancholy Eeyore,

and the admirable hero of the book, Owl? The answers
to these questions might stun the "critics" into silence
for years!

Another promising project is that of enumerating and
glossing the strictly local elements in *Winnie-the-Pooh.*
It is obvious that when Milne refers to "a small spinney
of larch trees," he is not indulging in that irresponsible
"universality" that your New Critic finds everywhere,
but is being specific and definite. What is a larch tree, and
exactly which spinney of them did Milne have in mind?
Where is the "Hundred-Acre Wood"? Has it been bull-
dozed for lower-class slum projects and such poppycock,
or is it still in proper condition for a literary pilgrimage?
I spoke a moment ago of Owl: what kind of Owl was he
—the *Bubo virginianus,* the *Nyctea nyctea,* or the *Tyto
alba pratincola?* Are kangaroos and tigers commonly
found in A. A. Milne's little corner of England, or has
the author used his "poetic license" to borrow them from
some less inhabited district of the Isles? What meteoro-
logical conditions produce the seasonal flooding of what
stream, and what combinations of geosyncline, glacial
detritus, and subsoil would have produced the variety of
trees, rocky places, bogs, sandy pits, and mounds that we

find within this limited area? [2] Shepard's map no doubt provides us with an interesting, albeit crude, start in this direction, but the literary detective can hardly complain that all his work has been done for him in advance!

Next, there is the matter of *Winnie-the-Pooh*'s literary antecedents. A complete survey of all previous children's literature would of course be *de rigueur* in any scholarly preface to a definitive edition. Where did Milne borrow from tradition; where was he "original" (i.e. where did he draw from sources that cannot be identified); and where, by the magic of his art, did he transmute traditional elements in the alembic of his imagination? Nor can we neglect the place of *Winnie-the-Pooh* in Milne's own career. The careful student, having noted that the two *Pooh* books are each preceded by a volume of nursery poems, will find innumerable points of continuity and development in the handling of "Edward Bear." I can envisage pages and pages of charts showing the gradual adding and subtracting of features in the conception of this character—all quite preliminary, *bien entendu*, to discussing what the character actually does in any one version. This must be left to future generations, who will thank our memories for laying, as I say, the scholarly groundwork for criticism.

As for the text itself, to the dull eye of a layman it might seem to offer disappointingly few cruxes to tax the literary detective's powers of cautious conjecture. It will come as no surprise to this audience, however, when

---

2 Professor Force does not mention the possibility that the mounds (which I am momentarily unable to locate in *Winnie-the-Pooh*) might be druidic ruins connected with a burial cult. I hope he will excuse my temerity in adding this suggestion, but I feel sure that he would have encouraged us to look into this if he had thought of it in time.—Ed.

I declare that *Winnie-the-Pooh*, like all other books, is positively fraught with thorny problems—the solving of which, in my opinion, must constitute the necessary clearing-away of land before your New Critic may be allowed to build his fantastic "structures" of Concrete Universals, or is it Universal Concretes? [Laughter.] I have had my team of graduate students working night and day on *Winnie-the-Pooh*, and we have come up with some fascinating questions you will want to have *your* graduate students answer. Thus, for instance, why are there no watermarks in *Winnie-the-Pooh*? Why are there no chain lines? Why no colophon? Why no catchwords? No signature? No cancelland or cancellans?

Now you will ask, are there out-and-out errors in the text of *Winnie-the-Pooh*? I hope you will pardon me if I smile in reply. Compared to this book, a First Quarto *Hamlet* is bibliographically uninteresting! In the first place, my students could not help noticing obvious discrepancies between the illustrations and the text. In the North Pole chapter, for instance, your symbolic-journey critics have failed to see that the official sign of discovery reads "DISCOVERED" in the text and "DICSOVERED" in Shepard's drawing. Which is correct? All further remarks about this chapter must wait upon the publication of Milne's complete correspondence with Shepard, Shepard's with Milne, Milne's with the publisher, the publisher's with Shepard, Shepard's with the publisher, and everyone's with the printer. I am not saying that this will clear up the difficulty; but I do mean that our hands are tied, critically speaking, until such time as this is done. That Milne and Shepard could be at loggerheads over fundamental questions like this one is demonstrated by two poems from *Now We Are Six*, "The Engineer"

and "Furry Bear." In both cases Milne evidently has none
of the "Pooh" characters in mind, yet in each the perhaps
overambitious Shepard works them into the illustration.
Here we have, you see, a whole new field of investigation
opening up before our eyes. Our decision to say that
"*the*" *Winnie-the-Pooh* is only Milne's, only Shepard's,
more Milne's than Shepard's, more Shepard's than Milne's,
both's or neither's, depends on what we learn about the
terms of collaboration, the temporal precedence of text
over pictures or vice versa, and similar factors. In the
meantime, the only scholarly thing for us to do is to look
at neither the text nor the pictures, for fear of receiving
impressions that might later prove to have been un-
canonical.

A different and more gripping class of textual problems
is offered us by simple misprints, which, however, we
may well hesitate to call "simple" when we have properly
evaluated them. Thus on page 68 of the Methuen *House
at Pooh Corner* (1928) we see that a close-quotation
mark is missing, while on page 93 we find an extra one
where it seems not to belong. Either error in isolation
would spur us to make the seemingly appropriate dele-
tion or addition, naturally not omitting to provide
the requisite explanatory textual apparatus. Taken together, on the other hand, the two errors oblige us to
suspect a mutual connection; if the one extra mark is
removed and then replaced at the earlier point where
one is missing, *voilà!* the Ur-text is restored. This sug-
gests that the reverse of the restorative process may actually have occurred in the typesetting; that, in other
words, the piece of type that wrongly found its way to
page 93 could be the very one that somehow dropped
out of page 68. To verify this we would need, of course,

access to all Milne's manuscript drafts and printer's type-
script as well as the galleys and page proofs, plus variorum Hinman readings from all other printed editions,
not to mention the complete cooperation of Methuen &
Company. After such excitement as this, I hope it will
not be too much of a disappointment if I tell you that I
have already assigned this project to one of my own
graduate students for his doctoral dissertation. [Murmurs
of "Too bad!" "Dash the luck!"] Within six or seven
years, in any case, we may find that this piece of groundwork for criticism has been laid.

Less dramatic, no doubt, are a further series of cruxes
to which we must nevertheless lend our patient attention.
I am thinking of miscellaneous inconsistencies, not so
much in the text as in the general plan of the story. Both
the text and the illustrations agree, for example, that Pooh
is well supplied with jars of honey, ingenuously mis-
spelled "HUNNY." Now, the source of this supply
would certainly be worth studying—perhaps a survey of
beekeeping practices in England in the 1920's would cast
some light on the problem—but we are also obliged to
consider how the word "HUNNY" arrived on each of
these jars. Surely this is not the manufacturer's spelling!
[Laughter.] Nor can it be the analphabetic Pooh's. Is it
Christopher Robin's, you say? But Pooh has these jars
from the very beginning, and it is clear that Christopher
Robin's spelling at this stage is insufficient to produce
the near-perfect "HUNNY." Before we go off into
metaphysical-critical speculations as to the meaning of this
anomaly, we should simply examine the possibility that
Milne failed to ponder the matter through as well as I
have done. If this proves to be so, it will not make us
think any the less of Milne's art—every book, after all,

endears itself to us through offering a few harmless er- rors to investigate—but it *will* prevent us from canting about "patterns of meaning" and similar rot.

This point also holds, I must say, for other as yet un- solved puzzles in the text: the discrepancies in the charac- ters' ages (Piglet is only three, but is treated more or less as an equal by the evidently aging Rabbit, Owl, and Kanga); the question of whether the characters have "grown up" in any sense from *Winnie-the-Pooh* to *The House at Pooh Corner* (microscopic comparative measurements of Shepard's drawings might provide a clue); and the general matter of relative misspellings by the unequally skilled spellers in the cast. It does seem a shame, doesn't it, that we should have at our command the most modern tools of research, not only microfilm readers and collating machines but giant electronic brains as well, and then fail to use them for want of problems that lend themselves to filing on coded cards? This business of misspellings may be just what we have been looking for! Every word written by Milne's characters ought to be fed into the machine, cross-referenced for age of misspeller, point in story, degree of misspelling, intended meaning, "unintentionally" suggested meaning, degree of similarity to other misspellings, and possible anagrams. Literally *millions* of data would then be avail- able for analysis by our graduate students, and our own duty as supervisors would be simplified to the task of helping the students re-insert their findings into the ma- chine. Perhaps—who knows?—the misspellings in *Pooh* will demonstrate cryptographically that the books were really written by Sir Francis Bacon! [3] [Chuckles and guffaws.]

3 Professor Force was, I believe, indulging in one of his noted

Well, gentlemen, this is the hopeful note on which I should like to take my leave of you this afternoon. As we see our colleagues, the physical scientists, crowding us ever farther away from the center of public respect, let us take heart, and learn a humble lesson from them: that modern research, if it is to be worthy of the name, must be *objective* research, reducible to graphs, charts, equations, formulae, ratios, correlations, indices, abbreviations, and percentiles. We old-timers, who have always been the only ones really to care for books, are better adapted to make the change-over to modern methods than is your fuzzy-headed "New Critic" with his mooning and drooling over symbolism. I leave you, gentlemen, with a message of progress and optimism. It is true that I want you to help me enforce a twenty-year moratorium on further emetic "critical studies" of *Pooh*, but I also trust that you will return to your universities with a sense that, bibliographically and scientifically speaking, we are on the threshold of the GOLDEN AGE OF *POOH!* [Applause.]

---

flights of humor here. Shortly after his talk was delivered, however, cryptographic evidence *was* adduced to show that the *Pooh* books were written not, of course, by Bacon but by Rudyard Kipling, who is alleged to be still alive today. See Prester S. Peacock, *The Man Who Was Milne* (Wichita: Personal Think Press, 1963). As reviews of this volume have not yet appeared, your editor may be excused for not assessing it prematurely in these pages.—Ed.

QUESTIONS AND STUDY PROJECTS

1. As a first exercise in the methodology Professor Force so eloquently defends, search through this Casebook for possible misprints. Report your findings, if any, to E. P. Dutton, 201 Park Avenue South, New York 3. Your research may help to improve subsequent editions of this text, in addition, of course, to laying the groundwork for criticism in your own career.

2. In the question period after Professor Force's lecture your editor made so bold as to ask him, "Sir, what is the latest thinking on whether *The House at Pooh Corner* should be included, as has been the loose practice of scholars hitherto, under the 'blanket' name of *Winnie-the-Pooh?* Must we not, upon investigating all the significant differences between the two volumes, adopt some more precise method of reference, such as *Winnie-One* and *Winnie-Two?*" Because of a time limitation Professor Force was unfortunately unable to reply. The question, however, may serve one of the more ambitious students in your class as a topic for a term paper.